TO HELP YOU *HEAL*

TO HELP YOU *HEAL*

Transform Your Life through the
Partnership of Faith, Psychology, & Grit

Marie Monville

To Help You Heal
Transform Your Life through the Partnership of Faith, Psychology, & Grit
Copyright ©2023 by Marie Monville, all rights reserved.

ISBN:
979-8-9891695-1-1 (print)
979-8-9891695-2-8 (ebook)
979-8-9891695-3-5 (audio)

Unless otherwise indicated, Scripture quotations are from The ESV® Bible (The Holy Bible, English Standard Version®), copyright © 2001 by Crossway, a publishing ministry of Good News Publishers. Used by permission. All rights reserved.

Scripture quotations marked MSG are taken from The Message, copyright © 1993, 2002, 2018 by Eugene H. Peterson. Used by permission of NavPress. All rights reserved. Represented by Tyndale House Publishers.

No portion of this book may be reproduced in any form without written permission from the publisher or author, including photocopy, recording, or any information storage and retrieval system now known or to be invented, without permission in writing from the publisher, except by a reviewer who wishes to quote brief passages in connection with a review written for inclusion in a magazine, newspaper, website, or broadcast. The web addresses referenced in this book were live and correct at the time of the book's publication but are subject to change.

This publication is designed to provide accurate and authoritative information regarding the subject matter covered. It is sold with the understanding that neither the author nor the publisher is engaged in rendering therapeutic, religious, medical, or other professional services. While the publisher and author have used their best efforts in preparing this book, they make no representations or warranties with respect to the accuracy or completeness of the contents of this book and specifically disclaim any implied guarantees for a particular purpose. The advice and strategies contained herein may not be suitable for your situation. You should consult with a professional when appropriate. Neither the publisher nor the author shall be liable for any loss or damages, including but not limited to special, incidental, consequential, personal, or other damages related to information provided.

Contact marie@mariemonville.com regarding bulk purchase discounts.

Library of Congress Control Number: 2023917952

Book cover: Kristen Ingebretson
Interior layout design/typesetting: Lisa Parnell
Copy/proofreading editor: Amanda Varian

To My Family — Thank you for listening, encouraging, and championing me throughout this process. You're the reason I've gotten this far.

To Heather Z. and Kelli C. — Your encouragement always came at the right time. Thank you for expressing your belief in me. I treasure your friendship.

Contents

Introduction	1
Chapter 1: Mind over Mindset	7
Chapter 2: Transforming Negative Self-Talk	19
Chapter 3: Understanding Self-Sabotage	33
Chapter 4: Courage to Dream	45
Chapter 5: Cue the Celebration	55
Chapter 6: Introductions	67
Chapter 7: Overcoming Our Trauma-Based Perspective	79
Chapter 8: Choosing Forgiveness	91
Chapter 9: Developing an Action Plan	103
Chapter 10: Persevering through the Middle	113
Chapter 11: Resilience and Determination	123
Chapter 12: Defying Limitations	135
Chapter 13: Before and After	145
Chapter 14: Fight for the Blessing	157
Chapter 15: Shine Your Light	169
Conclusion	181
Acknowledgments	187
Notes	191

Introduction

My Friend,

I see your pain, I feel your frustration, and I know your brokenness. You are not alone. We're different, but we're the same. You're desperate for healing and deeply desire transformation. But more than anything, you need a friend—someone to listen, encourage, and walk you through the valley. Because right now, you're not sure you will make it.

In the darkest places of my journey, I've felt it too. Life rarely goes the way we planned. It never looks like a Hallmark movie. We feel disappointed that this is what it means to be an adult. It's certainly not what we imagined. No one told us it would be hard, and we feel isolated in our brokenness. We face secret struggles and hide our agony behind a façade of fake confidence. It isn't the life we want. We feel abandoned in the place where we need help most. Grief and disappointment are our closest companions.

I lost my first daughter at 26 weeks of pregnancy when I was twenty. I had an ectopic pregnancy about a year later. My grandparents died before I was ready to lose their influence. My father died due to lung cancer when he was sixty-one. And my first husband committed the Amish schoolhouse shooting when I was twenty-eight. We had three young children at the time. I became a single mom and a widow in one overwhelming moment. None of that sounds like a successful storyline for someone's life or an episode of any show I'd want to watch.

And maybe you feel the same when you look across the landscape of your life. There's no "happily ever after" or tidy wrap-up to difficult circumstances within a sixty-minute time frame. Your problems span seasons, years, and decades. You feel like it's just one thing after another. You have difficulty enjoying the "good moments" because you're holding your breath for the next all-consuming situation inevitably headed your way. You wish life could play out like a Hallmark movie, but you don't even believe you can find a happy ending anymore. You're tired of fighting and sometimes wonder if it's worth it. When you look at life and think about the journey that's brought you here, it's a painful reminder—nothing went the way you planned. Don't feel guilty about those thoughts. Feel the feelings. Telling yourself you must be strong and push the pain aside is not the path to healing.

I understand. I've battled the same emotions and had the same thoughts. In the months after losing my first daughter, I tried to tell myself I would feel better if I stayed busy and appeared capable, but it was a lie. I volunteered, went back to work, and struggled through most days, knowing I wasn't strong or capable. I was miserably trying to stay afloat in a raging sea of pain. Most days, I felt like I was drowning in my brokenness. If I could go back and do it differently, I'd surround myself with a robust support system willing to acknowledge that the only path to healing is one which walks through pain.

And because of this, I'm not going to try to sell you some system of false beliefs based on manifesting a positive outlook for your life. I'm not attempting to convince you that your brokenness will make you stronger. And I don't want you to buy into the lie that this stuff was always God's best plan for you. Others have done these things to me, and it was a brutal assault. Inferring that pain is God's plan strips away the very essence of our humanity. It relegates tragedy and brokenness to life lessons and stands in opposition to the deep, targeted healing we need if we ever hope to move past it.

When we buy into the lie that all this pain is "for our good," it doesn't matter what perspective we try to embrace to make us feel better; it won't last. Distractions, self-medicating with substances, and self-help books from a guru with zero life experience fail to provide genuine, authentic change. And I don't know about you, but I can't do fake anymore. I don't want a temporary fix. If I'm going to invest myself in something, it can't be a waste of my time. I deserve more, and so do you. But let's back up a second. Before you think I'm anti-alcohol based on my statement that self-medicating with substances doesn't work, let me clarify. I don't think alcohol is evil. However, it's all about how we use it or our purpose for ingesting it. Anything that merely numbs my pain is doing me a disservice. I'm doing myself a disservice. It doesn't matter if it's with a chocolate chip cookie or an espresso martini. But let's dog-ear this topic and come back to it. I'm getting ahead of myself. The point is that we are the only ones who can change our life. We are the ones who hold the power needed to rise above our circumstances. And I hear your question, "How am I supposed to rise above any of this?" I feel your bitterness and skepticism, and it's okay if it's your starting point for this journey.

You and all your doubts are welcome here. Come as you are. Walk with me. I promise 100 percent honesty. Nothing less than an authentic version of what I've discovered. These are the truths I wish someone would have whispered in the difficult days of my journey. These are the words I've learned on the hard road, and I want to save you from traveling the same exhausting path. There are things we do to ourselves that make it more complicated than it needs to be. But we do them because no one has taught us any other way. Do you remember the list of less-than-stellar life experiences I described? I've learned how to live a life not defined by those events. Instead, I stand on top of my circumstances.

The other side to my story is this—I remarried seven months after the Amish schoolhouse shooting. The relationship I have with my husband, Dan, is an extraordinary gift—we've raised our blended family of five kids and adopted our youngest. I've had the opportunity to tell my story in a book I wrote (*One Light Still Shines*) and through various speaking engagements, blogs, and interviews. I'm a grandma, which is one of the best experiences of my life. My grandson calls me Lolli, and yes, my husband is Pop. In January 2020, just before the pandemic hit, I started college. I began with the goal of graduating in less than four years while maintaining straight A's. The overachiever in me had something to prove, more to myself than anyone else.

I started a coaching business while in college and navigating the world amid the pandemic. Since graduating from Immaculata University, I launched Elevated Solutions Consulting, where I help entrepreneurs and small businesses strengthen their organizations through a focus on strategy, human capital, and culture. But it's not just about the transformation of circumstance. It's what happened inside of me. I'm a different person than I was before I walked the hard road. Hardship made some of the difference, but a shift also happened despite the circumstances. It's what I found inside myself—the treasure buried deep within. I wouldn't have looked for otherwise.

I don't run at full speed into difficulty, assuming I can create a purposeful experience. I doubt myself and succumb to the negative voice in my head, but I've also learned I'm far more capable than I imagine. When I began college, I was nervous and didn't feel like I belonged. I remember sitting in class, feeling like an outcast because I was much older than everyone else. But I quickly realized the other students (and my professors didn't see me that way). They asked for my opinion and valued my input. And it made all the difference.

English 101 with Professor Aronovitz was my first class on my inaugural day of college. As I sat at my desk, he announced we would begin each session with a surprise writing prompt, followed by a few minutes to write, before sharing our response with the class. His words captivated my attention. I loved a challenge and enjoyed writing, but the thought of sharing my work with the rest of the class brought a shockwave of stress. I took a deep breath, tightened the grip on my pencil (so my hands stopped shaking), and waited for our first writing assignment. "Discuss something you would fight for even if it means standing up to authority." The words flowed as I focused on adoption advocacy, specifically the adoption of older children. When our writing time ended, Professor Aronovitz asked for volunteers, and I avoided eye contact—so did the rest of my class. A small part of my brain wanted to volunteer, but I didn't want to go first. I was waiting to judge myself against one of my classmate's works and judge our professor's response. After a short lecture on class participation, another student volunteered to read her entry. Professor Aronovitz encouraged her and interjected relevant information regarding her topic; he didn't criticize. I expected criticism. As he asked for another volunteer, I nervously raised my hand and read my journal entry. He praised the structure of my essay and the way I backed up my feelings with facts. In those brief moments, he gave me the courage to believe I would successfully conquer his class and enjoy the process.

Hardship births courage, and when surrounded by the right people, it produces joy. I love my life, who I am, and who I'm still becoming, but I would not have purposefully chosen it. No one would want this. As I've allowed God to walk me through it, He's shown me how to use the tools I'll share with you, to stand on top of my circumstances. And you can stand on top of yours too. I believe it even if you don't. I'll carry you until you can walk alone because I want more for you than you know right now. You have a purpose. There are dreams, goals, and secret desires locked inside your heart. Maybe they are buried so deep that you don't even know they exist. You deserve to find them.

It's time for your transformation. I'm here for you; you are my sole concern. You have value and worth. You have skills and abilities that, when tapped into, will thrill you. If you're frustrated by the context of your existence, then you're in the right place because we're going to do something about it. This book contains the tools which enable us to solve our challenges and the strategies necessary to cultivate a life we love.

When someone who has already walked a similar road shares their wisdom, we benefit from their hard-earned shortcut. It's like playing Candyland. I remember the look on my kids' faces when they turned over a card that enabled them to jump ahead—pure joy and the assurance they would win. But other cards seem to slow us down or cause us to lose a turn. And that's the way life often works. We never know what we'll get until we turn the card over. Sometimes we get the shortcut, but sometimes we're delayed, or worse yet, we lose a turn.

Maybe you're stuck due to someone else's choices. Your current situation was not directly due to your actions but the card you received. Or perhaps you're stuck because you want to avoid turning over another bad card. You're just sitting there, refusing to take your turn. It's okay to admit you want to prevent the possibility of additional pain. Maybe you're stuck because someone offered "well-meaning advice" that made everything worse. I understand because I've been there too. And since I know your pain, I can't leave you here. In the following pages, I'll tell you more about myself, my struggles, and how I overcame them. Because if I can do it, you can too. Come with me. Take my hand. It's time to go. You're not alone—let's do this together.

Chapter 1
Mind over Mindset

The basic premise of "mind over matter" is that human beings can control their circumstance, problem, and environment through the power of their mind. Sir Charles Lyell described the idea of mind over matter in the late 1700s. However, since then, many other philosophers, authors, and religious figures have incorporated the phrase into their belief structure. I don't know about you, but I struggle to buy into the concept because it only applies to some situations. I can control my actions through the power of my mind when thinking about why I should not eat the whole container of fudge on my kitchen counter. But I can't use the power of my mind to transform circumstances surrounding pain, loss, and brokenness. I can change my perspective or beliefs (my mindset) but not the physical problem. Maybe the phrase should say "Mind over Mindset."

We define mindset as "a set of beliefs that shape how you make sense of the world and yourself. It influences how you think, feel, and behave in any given situation." But I prefer to say it this way: perspective is everything. Whatever I believe about myself and a given outcome becomes my reality. When I lost my first daughter, I was devastated. There are almost no words capable of expressing the profound sorrow I felt and the overall destruction of the life I had envisioned.

While pregnant, most expectant mothers and fathers begin to dream about their children. What color hair/eyes will they have? Will they have more of their mother or father's personality? We create a storyline as we plan the experiences we will share with them. We step into the joy we've imagined. When you lose a child, you lose the future you've envisioned. It's all-encompassing. When my daughter died, my dreams and hopes died with her. I had not prepared for life without her, and I was lost. I remember telling myself I couldn't do this. I could not imagine surviving this loss. I couldn't figure out how to heal or find hope for the future. I cried every day for months. Several times a week, I drove forty-five minutes to visit my mom at work because I couldn't stand being in my empty house and didn't know what else to do. The silence was deafening. And you know what happens when something is wrong, and you see your mom? I cried at her work—every single time. I could not control these circumstances or bring my daughter back. And at that point in my life, I didn't realize I could influence my mindset. In some ways, though, I did control it. I told myself I couldn't do this, and I was right.

And then, where you'd least expect it, I experienced a different outcome. I walked through the aftermath of the Amish schoolhouse shooting almost ten years later. My husband took the schoolhouse hostage, killed five young girls, wounded five more, and killed himself. (You can read more about my story in my first book, *One Light Still Shines*.) I felt an enormous weight as I thought about the families who woke up on a beautiful autumn morning and sent their kids to school, never knowing it would be the last time they saw them. The impact was catastrophic. Our community was devastated. I could not envision how I would lead my children through this season. The thought of waking up to this reality every morning for the rest of my life was incomprehensible. And yet, there was a glimmer of hope.

Over the previous ten years, I deepened my relationship with God. He met me in my brokenness. I talked to him about the pain I felt after losing my daughter. I began to feel His presence, but this was a new concept. Growing up, I attended church weekly, but we didn't learn about walking in constant communication with God. As I read the Bible in my young adult years, I was captivated by the way God stepped into each person's life. He spoke to many of them directly (Adam and Eve), some through objects (like Moses and the burning bush), and many through other people (Esther and her relationship with Mordecai). I wanted to believe that if God spoke to them, He would talk to me, but I struggled with doubt. Who was I to think He would *want* to talk with me? This question plagued my mind, but I couldn't push away the deepened desire for relationship. I wondered how others learned to hear His voice. And then, I began to think about it from the perspective of a parent and child. I wanted to talk with my kids. I loved hearing their voice when they started speaking; I cherished every laugh and mispronunciation. I couldn't help but smile as they responded to the sound of my voice. And if these experiences mattered to me, they had to matter to God.

This perspective was the first step in the process of changing my mindset. As I found the courage to believe God wanted to hear my voice and was delighted in my desire to listen to Him, I began to hear Him. I challenged myself to look for other ways He invested in my life, and the more I looked, the more I saw Him. These experiences came through simple daily prayers asking for parenting wisdom, help to build a relationship with my husband and extended family, and opportunities to serve others. As I prayed, believing God heard me and would respond, I felt His guidance. I saw how He opened doors to lead a weekly women's ministry, brought connection with my family, and gave me strategies as I parented our children. I continually told myself, "God is speaking to me, and He will help me." And He did. My doubt shifted to belief as I changed my mindset.

I wasn't aware of the mindset shifts that occurred throughout the nine years between losing my daughter and the Amish schoolhouse shooting, but I can see them now. As I walked through the aftermath of the shooting, I believed God would help me. And more than just me, I believed He would help everyone impacted by Charlie's choices. As hard as the season was, I was not lost. I felt God give me strength, and it transformed me. There were many things I did not want to do—frequent meetings with police detectives, burial preparations with the funeral home coordinator, and constantly refusing interview requests from relentless reporters. Even though I did not want to do it, I knew I could do it.

Change requires participation, but it doesn't begin and end with me. Don't get me wrong; countless individuals have changed their mindset without the influence of religion. Still, I believe the most impactful change comes from incorporating aspects of psychology with faith in God.

So how do we change our mindset? For me, it starts with a mental inventory. I spend some time thinking about my overall perspective. Is it positive or negative? Am I expecting good experiences or outcomes in my life? If I realize I'm struggling to maintain a positive perspective, I ask myself why? I can often trace generalized negativity back to an event (or many occasions) when I was disappointed. If left unchecked, disappointment can lead to cynicism.

Cynicism twists the positive into a passive-aggressive form of negativity. Here's how it plays out in my life. I'm a private person, and it has been challenging to cultivate friendships after the Amish schoolhouse shooting. I'm reserved when it comes to the personal details of my life. And sometimes, my history is too complicated—those who initially seemed friendly backed away once they connected to my story. I've had to protect myself from those who want a story, not an investment in my family. But I'll entrust myself to a friend willing to invest in me.

A decade ago, I thought I had found this friend. I listened, encouraged, and provided support. I believed she would do the same for me, but when I reached out, she dismissed my needs and refocused the conversation on her problems. And it became a pattern. Whenever I reached out, she manipulated the conversation, and I felt compelled to serve her instead. (Side note, I don't think she was malicious or selfish, I can see now that she wanted my support and not a friendship.) However, at the time, I became resentful. And then, my passive-aggressive (indirectly negative) perspective told me this would happen with all my current and future friendships. So, I stop reaching out, not just to this friend, but to all my friends. I was disappointed, but instead of dealing with my disappointment directly and telling myself this was not a healthy friendship, I became resentful and wrote off friendships in general.

> Change requires participation, but it doesn't begin and end with me.
> ... I believe the most impactful change comes from incorporating aspects of psychology with faith in God.

A few weeks later, another friend asked if I was okay; she realized we hadn't spoken in almost a month and wondered if she had done something wrong. Her phone call broke through my negative mindset. While it wasn't hard to correct my mindset, I've since realized this experience is one of my default responses to disappointment. I agree with the negative assumptions. I allow my thoughts to run unchecked, on repeat, through my mind. And the most dangerous part is this: I became so accustomed to the negativity that it became a foundational part of my routine.

To create change, I had to adjust my mindset. I needed to do more than view this friendship differently or revise my beliefs about relationships; I had to deal with the generalized discouragement I had welcomed into my mind. I began to agree with the negativity and created an environment where it stayed. It was as if this negative mindset had become my best friend. I trusted the negativity, and in some ways, I embraced it because negativity was a safe space. Living in a negative mindset does not result in unexpected disappointment. It was my protection mechanism. If I agreed with the negativity and created room for it to "move in" and get cozy—it would multiply. Negativity is like a couple of rabbits living in a hole under your bushes. At first, they are cute, and you should probably evict them, but it seems like they're not hurting anything, so you let them stay. And you become so accustomed to seeing them you almost forget they are there. But then suddenly, one morning a few months after you first saw them, you look out the window and realize they have taken over your entire yard. There are dozens of them. And you're kicking yourself for not taking steps to get rid of them a few months ago. You know it will be much more complicated now and require consistency over time. It's not a quick fix.

And the same is true when we're trying to change our mindset. The longer we've allowed the discouragement to reign, the harder it will be to correct it. It requires consistency over time, and you must have a plan. The good news is you can change your mindset. There is an endless array of options; you can find a comprehensive list online. Most don't require any special tools and won't cost a dime. Here are some suggestions:

- listen to uplifting podcasts or audiobooks
- find a friend you can meet with regularly for face-to-face encouragement
- pick up a hobby you enjoyed as a child
- journal
- engage in artistic expression

- take walks outdoors while noticing your surroundings
- revamp your internal dialogue (we'll dive deeper into this in a few chapters)

All these require intentional effort, and some of what you prefer depends on your personality and general preferences. Pick one that sounds fun (from my list or your online search) and try it. The thing is, though, it's not a one-time event. You're going to need consistency over time. Make it a part of your daily (or weekly) routine. I hear your question, "How much time will this take?" And before you tell me you can't make space for one more thing, I'll relieve your stress—start with ten to fifteen minutes. That's it. You don't need to block out an hour, but you might want to once you begin to see its impact.

Walking while listening to worship music is my favorite way to institute a mindset shift. It's beneficial to get out of my house (especially since I work from home), immerse myself in nature (regardless of the weather), and allow God to speak. Sometimes I'm ready for a walk the moment I start to feel discouraged, but other times I must force myself to do it. I don't always want to do what I know will benefit me. Often, I'll ask my dog, Bruno, if he wants to go for a walk. The moment I say the "w" word, I know he will keep me accountable. But I'm better for it. Deep breaths of fresh air, birds fluttering from one tree to another, and squirrels teasing Bruno just out of his reach make me laugh. As I laugh, it's impossible to stay discouraged. The song blaring through my AirPods further impacts my heart and mind; it brings positive expressions of truth to my negativity and becomes the theme I'll focus on throughout the day. And it all happens in ten minutes or less. It's life-changing, but only when I engage in it.

Keep an open mind as you embrace your activity; trust me when I say it's counterproductive to tell yourself "this isn't going to work." I've learned this the hard way, and I was right. It was pointless if I wasn't willing to be objective and analyze after—instead of before. Our culture conditions us to expect instantaneous results. We dismiss whatever we've attempted if we feel it has not garnered a significant impact after the first try. But that's not the way real progress works. Before analyzing potential progress, I must invest myself regularly, consistently, and without preconceived judgments.

And here's what happens as we intentionally invest in meaningful activities. We place value on ourselves. We prove to ourselves we are worth the commitment. It's easy to relegate ourselves to last place. We often live our lives focused on other people (family, friends, colleagues) or things (job, church, volunteer commitments) and tell ourselves we will engage in personally meaningful activities once we accomplish everything else. But here is the truth: if we have placed ourselves last, we will never get to anything personally beneficial because something else will always find its way onto our list. If we want to shift our mindset, we will have to carve out time (daily) to work on it. It's never going to happen on its own. And if you need other reasons to reinforce its importance, consider your stress level. We often wear stress as if it's a badge of honor. We resign ourselves to the fact that stress is a part of daily life, and we expect it to be a part of our adult experience. However, we are wrong.

Stress tells us something is out of balance. For too long, we've thought of stress management as massages, pedicures, an afternoon on the golf course, or some other "reward." But we need to shift our perception of stress management to our mindset. When we work to change from a negative to a positive (or negative to neutral) mindset, it will reduce our stress level. Stress has negative consequences on all areas/systems within our body. Stress lowers immune function, can cause digestive issues, and puts us at risk for cardiovascular conditions. Stress can exacerbate anxiety and depression.

Psychological studies have proven the positive impact of mindset work. We know these strategies are beneficial, but when I combine mindset-boosting activities with faith in God, the results increase exponentially. Since spending time in nature is one of my favorite mindset activities, you'll find me on the wooded walking path near my house most days from mid-March through November. I can walk along the path embracing one of several different perspectives, and each one provides a different outcome. I can walk, head down, focus on the trail, mind fixed on all the things I need to do when I get home or situations causing stress. This approach is the least beneficial. Instead, I can walk the path, looking at the trees, listening for birds, peering down at the adjacent creek hoping for a glimpse of the resident Blue Heron. I feel the anticipation as I approach the places where I usually see the heron, and even if I don't see it, I'll find some enjoyable takeaway. This perspective occurs because I took a break from my task-based circumstantial mindset. I might find a heart-shaped leaf on the ground, take a picture of a flower that captured my attention, or embrace the peace offered there as I stand still, eyes closed, breathing deeply in a space where I have zero responsibilities. This path does not depend on me. Maintaining the surroundings is not my job; I'm just there to breathe it in. I physically feel better after a walk on my beloved path.

But the ultimate impact comes when I invite God to walk with me on the path. I talk to Him about my stress. I tell Him about the exhausting situations in my life and the weariness that has settled over my soul. Then I ask Him to help me. I tell Him I need the reminder of His love and constant presence. And when I look down and see a heart-shaped leaf, it means something different. It's the answer to my prayer and brings a spark of hope to my heart. I feel compelled to nurture this tiny spark, and as I continue down the path, I search for further evidence of God's closeness. I find Him in the bird that flies directly in front of me, just a few feet from my face. I see His proof of the peace I need for this moment as the Blue Heron glides gracefully above the water's surface. I feel His whisper, "There's more. Trust Me for more," as I exit the path. I continue thinking about these experiences as I return home. And I wonder about the meaning behind His promise of more and His invitation to trust Him. This encounter with God stays with me the rest of the day. It comes back to my mind in one quiet second as I take the laundry out of the washer and stuff it in the dryer. I think about it later as I indulge in a hot bath at the end of the day. I close my eyes and return to the moment when I saw the heron gliding above the water. The heron infuses himself into my prayer, "God, I want to glide above the surface of these circumstances. Show me how to live like the heron." And then I remember God's promise, and I say, "Lord, help me to look for more, to trust You have more for me than what I know right now." I climb into bed and fall asleep with the by-product of a transformed mindset. Instead of anxious thoughts, I feel peace. My circumstances haven't changed, but I can set the stress aside and embrace a relationship with the God who meets me on the path and continues to walk with me.

My story isn't a recipe. You only need to find a wooded path if it's your thing too. God created us as unique individuals. We have five senses and a preference for specific types of interaction. We interpret the world around us and find joy in different ways. Just as there is an endless list of activities that will positively impact your mindset, there are endless ways to connect with God. He's not one-size-fits-most. Invite Him into your favorite activities. Pick your favorite, and then look for the ways God meets you. It is also beneficial to journal after spending time with Him. The conversation and interaction are impactful, and at the moment, I'm sure I will remember them forever. But I've found it's easy to get distracted or experience a stressful moment that sets me back later. When this happens, I forget the impact of time spent with

God, and it's lost (at least for a little while). You can spare yourself from this experience by taking a few minutes to write some notes about your interaction with Him.

I am frequently asked, "Why do I have difficulty hearing God when I'm praying at home?" Those experiencing this type of frustration feel like they cannot connect with God, even though they try to pursue a relationship with Him. They are doing their best to stay quiet and open to His voice, but they can't hear Him. When this situation happens frequently, it causes them to give up on the concept of prayer, negatively impacting their relationship with God because they feel ashamed they don't have a meaningful prayer life. They start to believe God doesn't want to talk with them. Can you relate? I can, and here's what I've found. It's difficult for me to concentrate when I sit still during times of prayer. However, connecting with God while walking on the path is easy.

You might find the same is true for you. When you're engaged in your favorite mindset activity or taking a shower, you can hear God without the hindrances that happen when you're trying to sit still. I'm not a licensed psychologist, but I've spent time researching the brain and why we have difficulty sitting to pray versus prayer while engaged in another activity. (Side note, if you're interested in more on this, check out Dr. Andrew Newberg, MD.) Each area of our brain processes a different type of activity or event. One area processes emotion (the amygdala), and another handles cognitive functions like memory and attention (the prefrontal cortex). The cerebellum helps to coordinate our movements. Generally, one area of the brain dominates the rest due to the activity, stress, or thought processes we are experiencing. For example, if I'm processing a highly emotional experience, my amygdala gets most of the brain power and focus. If I'm sorting through the steps to conquer a problem, task, or long-term scenario, then my prefrontal cortex is doing the work. And when these areas of my brain are engaged, it is hard for me to engage with God. My brain is so busy doing all this work that it can't receive any of God's messages. But when I'm engaged in a low-level activity, such as walking, my cerebellum gets a higher percentage of my brain's effort and output. This activity also minimizes the focus in regions such as the prefrontal cortex and amygdala. It's like the conditions researchers describe if you're trying to get into a state of "flow."

If you're struggling with prayer, think about a time when you were in a state of flow. Why not pair the activity with prayer? When we are seated, thinking about highly emotional experiences or decisions looming over our lives, our amygdala fires off, or our prefrontal cortex ignites. They are capitalizing on all our attention/focus, which is why it can feel hard to hear God. By engaging in some activity, we quiet those areas of our brain, allowing ourselves to connect with Him.

It's easy to feel bad about ourselves and assume we're the ones with the problem, but maybe we need to tweak our approach to our relationship with God. As a mom, I enjoy spending time with my kids. I love sharing experiences with them—not just the ones I like but the ones they appreciate. I believe it's the same with God. He loves spending time with us and engaging in things we enjoy. I don't enjoy sitting still for long periods in my regular life. It's easier for me to concentrate when my brain is fully engaged. So I must take this perspective into the way I approach prayer. The effectiveness of prayer is not dependent upon the context of my body. Seated prayer doesn't get God's attention better than the prayers I've spoken while walking. Recognizing and understanding the impact of this truth brings freedom. It's a significant mindset shift. I feel excited about spending time with God instead of feeling shame and frustration that our relationship isn't working. Before you turn the page, take some time to think about activities you could do with God. What activities do you enjoy? Where could you welcome Him to engage with you?

Chapter 2
Transforming Negative Self-Talk

According to the National Science Foundation, the average person has 12,000–60,000 thoughts per day. Of those thoughts, 80 percent are repetitive, and 95 percent are negative. There isn't an authoritative statistic on how many of the 12,000–60,000 thoughts are about ourselves. However, if 80 percent of our thoughts are repetitive and 95 percent are negative, these statistics have significant implications for our self-talk—it infers that we consistently reinforce negativity over the long term.

How would you describe your self-talk? What are some of the things you say about yourself? Are they statements like, "You're creative, capable, and you grow through every obstacle"? Or does it sound more like, "You give up so easily, you never speak up for yourself so it's no wonder you're resentful about your workload, and you're never going to lose twenty pounds because you can't keep five pounds off"? Here's the thing, most of us allow a level of cruelty in our self-talk that we wouldn't tolerate from anyone else.

I remember my negative self-talk when I think about my first English Composition 101 class. I didn't raise my hand because I was sure Professor Aronovitz would scrutinize my work. Before his class, I wasn't confident in my ability. (If you're wondering, I didn't tell him I had written a book.) I assumed he would see me the same way I saw myself, but he didn't. I changed my negative self-talk because I changed what I saw as the truth. I saw myself based on my struggles, the places where I felt like a failure, and areas where I knew growth was needed. And this experience wasn't confined to English 101. My college journey earned me a degree, but more than that, it changed what I believed about myself and gave me the confidence to take on everything since.

Often our negative self-talk has an element of truth, making it easy to believe. And so, we agree with the negativity, reinforcing it is the truth. And while it may be true that we give up easily, hesitate to speak up for ourselves, feel resentful about our workload, or have trouble keeping off five pounds, we can challenge the truth behind those statements. Let's think about it objectively. If I were talking with a friend who said, "I'm frustrated with myself; I give up so easily on any goal I want to go after." I would disagree with her; I would ask for more information. I would say something like, "Tell me what you mean." Let's assume the conversation went something like this:

> Friend: "Well, three weeks ago, I decided I wanted to lose ten pounds in the next two months. Some of my outfits are uncomfortable because I've gained weight and need to get it off. I was consistent for a couple of days, but then it was the weekend, and I overslept, so I didn't do my workout. My husband wanted to go to dinner at our favorite Italian place, and between the garlic knots and tiramisu, I blew all the progress I had made during the week. Then Saturday rolled into Sunday, and I haven't gotten back on track."

I would not tell her she was a failure. I'd say, "Oh yes, I understand that feeling. It's hard to stick with goals when carbs are involved. Let's do it together. Accountability is everything." I wouldn't walk away from the conversation thinking she was a quitter and wouldn't ever reach her goal. I would feel compassion toward her, and then I would think about how our partnership would help fuel her success and the benefit I would receive in return. But we don't challenge ourselves to see more than the negativity. We use the truth like a weapon and destroy ourselves with it.

What if, instead of using truth to destroy, we used it to strengthen? If we know our weaknesses, we can identify areas needing extra attention. If it's hard to resist the temptation incurred at our favorite Italian restaurant, we pick a different place to eat. We can use the truth to set ourselves up for success instead of expecting (and welcoming) failure. If it's challenging to speak up for ourselves (at home or work) and we end up with an enormous workload, it's likely due to our well-meaning care of those around us. And the people our workload benefits probably have no idea we are overwhelmed. If they knew the weight we experience when saying yes to things that shouldn't be our responsibility, they would feel bad. If it's hard to say no, we can work toward it by taking steps.

- Step 1: We work toward a partnership instead of our sole responsibility. When asked to do something outside our typical workload, we can say, "I don't mind helping you but can we do it together?"
- Step 2: We move from a partnership to their ownership. When they ask the next time, we can say, "I'm busy right now, but I'll check back with you in an hour or so; if you're still having trouble with it, I can help then."

- Step 3: We say no. "I'm sorry, but I can't do it right now." We build up to "no" in pieces, which benefits the other person and us. We gain confidence in our ability to say no, and they learn to do it themselves.

Positive self-talk is often more subjective. Statements like, "I'm creative, I learn from every obstacle, or I'm capable of every task that comes my way" isn't based on fact. They are opinions. And even if we occasionally interject them through our internal dialogue, they carry a lesser impact than a fact-based statement. It's hard to find positive things to say about ourselves. We experience this when we write a bio—for our LinkedIn profiles, a company website, or even our Instagram accounts. It's often challenging to think of positive, fact-based statements. Sometimes we write them, and we don't believe them. But when we can only conjure up a subjective (opinion-based) statement, it does not elicit the same response in our brain. It's as if our brain says, "You don't believe it's the truth because if you did, you'd actually stand on it, shout it, and unashamedly proclaim it to the world around you."

Why is it so hard to say good things about ourselves? It's not like we aren't capable of them. We've all had at least a few incredible, self-created moments in our lifetime. But we hold back from declaring them; we don't talk about them; instead, we can barely whisper them. For some of us, it's due to a faulty understanding of pride. Our culture or community has told us if we speak positive words about ourselves, talk about, or post about our successes, it is evidence of pride. Depending on our upbringing, the adults in our lives frequently reinforce this concept. While the Bible does say, "Pride goes before destruction, and a haughty spirit before a fall" (Proverbs 16:18), we can quickly take it out of context. But this verse doesn't mean every positive statement we make about ourselves equals an issue with pride.

Dictionary.com defines pride as "a high or inordinate opinion of one's dignity, importance, merit, or superiority, whether as cherished in the mind or as displayed in bearing, conduct, etc." Inordinate refers to something outside of normal limits. If you have an unusually high opinion of yourself outside the realm of what is typical for your level of accomplishment, then you might have a problem with pride. But most of us think we show prideful behaviors or thoughts when we dare to talk about one successful endeavor.

Let's look at it objectively. Think of something you have done well; you passed your driver's test on the first attempt, have never been in an accident, and have not received any speeding tickets. You are an exceptional driver. There's nothing wrong with making this type of statement, and since it is fact-based, it positively impacts your brain. You may be well-known in your circle of friends and family for your expertise in the kitchen. You create delicious dessert masterpieces, and everyone loves them. You are a highly skilled baker with an excellent reputation. Again, there's nothing prideful about this type of statement, and it's the truth (facts)!

If you struggle to come up with similar statements, ask a friend for help. It's always easier to identify positive attributes in others versus ourselves. Better yet, ask a few people whom you deeply trust. Write down their statements, speak their words, and allow their comments to influence you. You will feel the impact of this exercise. Grab a box of tissues, create space to process their affirmations, and settle them deep within your heart. Then once the words have settled, look for themes and build positive self-talk statements from this list.

But this brings up another problem—most of us need help handling compliments. It doesn't matter if the words focus on our cute T-shirt, how we conquered a difficult season with our kids, or a recent promotion. We discount it. I say, "Oh this old thing, I've had it forever. In fact, I got it on sale at Target for $5.00." Or "Totally God. I never could've done it on my own." While it's okay to admit we bought something on sale or God gave us strength when we were weak, we can do it in a way that doesn't take our involvement out of the compliment. We can acknowledge the wisdom God gave without minimizing our part in the outcome. We are glad we overcame the stressful season and didn't give up. We can say something as simple as "Thank you." When we discount compliments, we admit we don't believe those statements are true. This is why it's significant to hear positive feedback from others. When we have a relationship rooted in trust, we know they're not just trying to make us feel good. They are sincere, and they believe their words are valid. As we speak them over ourselves, we begin replacing our negative self-talk (half-truths) with the truth of their words. And it's a powerful shift.

Whether you ask a friend for input or come up with statements yourself, make sure they are fact-based. Write them out and place them where you will see the words frequently. If you want to take it to the next level, set a reminder on your phone, and say the statements aloud several times a day. Look at yourself in the mirror while you say them. You might feel silly at first but keep doing it. As you declare these words daily, your brain will feel the impact, and you will experience fewer negative thoughts. In my most recent season of college assignments, I started reading my professor's feedback over myself. Sometimes I printed their comments and hung them on my refrigerator. I wrote them in my journal, and I read them aloud. I felt silly; at first, I didn't want my family to see or hear me doing this exercise. But eventually, as my confidence and positive self-talk increased, I told them what my professors said. The comments from my professors changed me, but it wouldn't have occurred if I wasn't intentionally reinforcing the truth of their statements.

Utilizing these tools will help you reduce negative self-talk, but you can create a more profound transformation by partnering this practice with faith. Years ago, a mentor told me to ask God what He thought about me. My initial reaction was one of disbelief. I couldn't understand why I would want to hear what God thought. He knew all my failures. God was aware of every mistake I made, the insensitive comments I'd said, and the critical thoughts I'd had. Why would I want to ask what He thought of me? I couldn't imagine He would have anything positive to say.

I spent the following twenty-four hours arguing (with myself) about why this was a terrible and wonderful idea. But in the end, I trusted my mentor

> When we discount compliments, we admit we don't believe those statements are true.

more than my fears, and I followed her advice. I asked God what He thought about me. And then it was as if I sat there, head tilted away, eyes squinted, looking out of the corner of my left eye, waiting to see what He had to say but feeling sure it wouldn't be anything I wanted to hear. It's the way I felt in high school when a teacher passed back a big assignment. They laid the papers, face down, on our desks, and time stood still. There was no breathing; it was almost as if my heart stopped beating as I momentarily vacillated between wanting to know my grade and living in the bliss of not knowing.

But God isn't my high school teacher. He is not grading my life, looking for everything I've done wrong. He's not assessing my actions; He is building a relationship with me. So much of what I understand about God's love comes through the comparison of parenting. As a mom, I want my kids to know their strengths and the undeniable gifts within them. Yes, I know many of their flaws. I see the impact of their doubts, procrastination, and lack of follow-through. But I focus on something other than those things when I talk to them about what I've observed. If they could catch a glimpse of what's inside them, they would end self-doubt; my kids would feel motivated to tackle their goals and they would follow through in record time. God does the same with me. Instead of centering on my failures, He focuses on growth. He saw all the places where I had kept my heart open to Him, and those were the things He highlighted. I felt His kindness, compassion, and desire to show me more than my flaws. It wasn't hard to envision all the critical things He could say about me, but assuming He would provide positive feedback was challenging. As I met God in that moment, I realized I had felt unworthy, as if my self-perceived failures disqualified me from any positive recognition. His words impacted my present moment and wiped away my feelings of worthlessness from the past. I felt Him say I was "hitting it out of the park." I never expected God to infer I'd nailed a home run, but that's exactly what He said, and it changed me. It gave me confidence to believe I was doing this life well, despite all the challenges, trauma, and insecurity.

I was grateful for my mentor's challenge. And now, I want to pass her challenge along to you. It doesn't matter where you're at in your relationship with God. There are no prerequisites. If you have yet to initiate a conversation with Him, it's as simple as asking Him to help you hear His voice. There have been very few times when I've audibly heard God speak to me. Most often, it's a feeling. I can *feel* Him—I feel His presence and His perspective. Sometimes it's a tingly, relaxed sensation that travels through my body. Other times I feel highly emotional, and tears well up in my eyes. But often, there isn't a specific emotion accompanying His words—I just know it's Him.

But it wasn't always like that. I didn't grow up in a church where we learned how to hear God. I was encouraged to read my Bible, pray, and participate in weekly church services, but it felt more like a one-sided relationship—I talked, and (hopefully) He listened, but that's not what God wants. I don't want my kids to have a one-sided relationship with me. How would it feel to plan to talk with someone you cared about and wanted a relationship with, only to find they never engaged with you? How would you feel if they didn't make eye contact, nod, use any verbal/nonverbal cues, or respond in some way to your conversation? Once or twice of this experience and you'd probably stop pursuing the relationship. I wouldn't do this to my kids, and God doesn't do this to us, either.

I hear your question; if He's not silent, why don't we hear Him? Why didn't I hear a response or interjection of God's voice during those decades of growing up in church? There were three main reasons:

1. I wasn't taught to expect some interconnected relationship.
2. Since others told me to focus on all the reasons my sin had separated me from God, I didn't realize more than focusing on my sin, He wanted to focus on our relationship.
3. I wasn't taught how to hear Him.

After losing my first daughter, I knew I needed God in a different way than I'd experienced growing up. I needed more from Him. I felt like I was dying inside. The weight of grief was quietly crushing my soul. I began asking God to show up in my life in ways I could see or hear. I needed to know him as a friend. He gave more in relationship to the people I'd read about in the Bible than I had experienced. He talked to them, helped them, and demonstrated His care through friendship. If God pursued relationships with them, why wouldn't He do the same with me?

I needed to figure out where or how to start. I didn't have a formula or recipe to follow. Since I wasn't hearing God's voice, I needed to know how it worked. I asked God to help me hear His voice, and I kept asking. After several weeks of constant requests, with no input from God, I wondered if He even wanted to talk to me. And then a thought popped into my head, "Do you even believe I would want to talk to you?" My mind gave an automatic answer, "No." And I realized I was the problem. I didn't hear God because I didn't believe He wanted to talk to me. Why wouldn't I think God wanted to have a conversation with me? Because I wasn't special. I wasn't one of those famous biblical icons, and I wasn't brave like Esther or confident like Mary. They were extraordinary, while I was ordinary at best.

I've learned a lot since then. If I could go back and talk myself through that season, I would have said, "You're never going to find your worth based on comparison." The people we read about in the Bible were ordinary, just like you and me. We're the ones who give them catchphrases or qualifications we instinctively associate with their name. And no place in the Bible tells us we must measure up to their highlights. They made mistakes, they feared undesirable outcomes, and they needed encouragement. Some of them made decisions opposite of God's call. But God built a relationship with them anyway. That's the point—our relationship with God exists on the foundation of His love for us, not our qualifications. Are we living from a place of recognizing God loves us and wants to spend time with us? It's easier to hear His voice when the answer is "Yes."

If you think you want this type of relationship and believe God speaks, but you still find it hard to believe He's talking to you, here's a little more encouragement. In Matthew 11, we read a story about a father who stood face-to-face with Jesus. He knew Jesus was a healer. I don't know the backstory, but he either saw or heard evidence that caused him to believe Jesus could heal his son. However, as he stood there, looking at this man who had an incredible reputation for an unending stream of breathtaking miracles, he felt the impact of his doubts. He voiced the reality of the war waging within him, "I believe, but help my unbelief." Do you know what Jesus did? He healed the boy. Jesus did not lecture the father on his inability to trust. Jesus did not launch into some shame-inducing, passive-aggressive admonishment. Instead, Jesus did what He wanted to do; He loved the child and his father even though this father admittedly struggled with doubt.

I can relate to the father. And just as Jesus didn't expect perfection from that father, He does not expect it from you or me. My inability to hear God's voice came from my lack of belief that God would want to speak to *me*. He knew that Jesus could heal his child, but he didn't know if He would. During those weeks I spent asking God to help me hear His voice, I felt the same way. I knew God could speak to me, but I didn't know if He would. I believed, but I needed help to overcome my unbelief. And He helped me because He loves me. He loves you, and He will do the same for you. He wants a relationship with you and is speaking to you right now.

> You're never going to find your worth based on comparison.

It's hard to hear Him if I focus on one task after the next. If I can't pull my eyes away from my to-do list, there's not much room for God to make His way into my day. I'm not perfect. I don't have everything figured out. I have the tools, but sometimes I don't use them. Occasionally it's intentional. I have days when I'm discouraged, and I sit (miserably) in my feelings. But there are other days when I forget that I have these tools, and I don't stop long enough to remind myself. Have you ever searched for your glasses only to find that they were on your head? Or were you running around your house looking for your cell phone only to realize it was in your hand all along? For me, it's the same way with these tools. Sometimes I'm so busy getting through my day that I don't remember to use the things that make my navigation more successful.

We must pause long enough to identify that we are stuck, grab our tools, and change our mindset. We must remind ourselves of our previous (fact-based) successes or strengths that enabled us to reset our inner dialogue. But then, we add another dimension to our tools when we ask God to tell us what He thinks about us. If one of my children were unnecessarily hard on themselves, constantly berating their accomplishments, comparing themselves to their peers, and telling me that they wouldn't ever find success, I would feel heartbroken for them. I'd want them to know how strong and insightful they are and the potential I see inside them. And it's the same with God. He wants us to understand what He sees. He wants to share His words, but we must open our hearts and let Him in. God is unique, and so are we. He won't always speak the same way, but He *will* speak. We can start by believing that He wants to talk to us and then asking Him to help us hear His voice. And hearing His voice changes everything.

Throughout our journey, there are times when we need more than the tools I've offered to overcome the difficulties we're facing. If this happens, one of the best additional tools we can pick up is counseling from a mental health professional. And it's easier to schedule our first appointment if we know our options before we need them. Look for someone who has passed their licensure tests and certification requirements. They have extensive training and experience and are well-equipped to help you. And if, after a few appointments, you feel like it's not working, don't give up on therapy; instead, find a different professional. It's like getting your hair cut. Sometimes you find the perfect stylist who gets you on the first try. They intuitively know how to cut your hair and which styles will look best with your hair texture and face shape. But other times, you'll only sit in their chair once because they didn't listen, took it three inches shorter than you asked, and you don't want anyone to see you until it grows back (yes, that happened to me). Just as you wouldn't give up on getting a trim just because your previous stylist didn't cut your hair the way you wanted, don't give up on finding a therapist who is a good fit just because the last one didn't work out. We all need various tools in our toolbox, and sometimes it takes a few attempts to find the person best suited to our needs. We can overcome negative self-talk, and perhaps the most encouraging part is this—we're not alone. We all struggle with some aspect of negativity, even if it seems so normal, we're unaware it exists. As we work to shift into a more positive perspective, we'll see increases in our confidence, joy, ability to hear God, and willingness to go after our dreams. It's worth the work. You're worth the work.

Chapter 3
Understanding Self-Sabotage

As we work on our mindset and reframe our negative self-talk, we must also become aware of the way we self-sabotage. Self-sabotage is negative self-talk's BFF. They link arms and work together to tear us down, and often we participate in their schemes. I'm my own worst enemy. When I think about obstacles to my success, I'd much rather say it was something or someone that became a barrier to forward progress, but it's my fault. I can't tell you how many things I've talked myself out of doing. Maybe you can relate. I could fill at least two solid pages with scenarios (big and small) where I decided the better choice was not to move forward. The moment a new idea occurs in my brain, and I begin to engage in the concept, the ulterior part of my being starts to list all the reasons why this is a terrible suggestion. For me, self-sabotage sounds like, "I can't do this. I'm not strong enough. I don't have the necessary skill set. I'm not confident. I'm too tired. I have too many other things to do." Self-sabotage goes after the hard things; it's never the easy ones. I'll self-sabotage my effort to reduce or eliminate sugar from my diet, but I won't self-sabotage a desire to eat chocolate every day.

I've self-sabotaged my diet and exercise goals, my daily routines (going to bed early), projects and ministries I've thought about starting. I can see the beginnings of self-sabotage in the way I hesitated to raise my hand all the way back in elementary school. I didn't join sports teams, try out for our high school choir, or other extracurricular clubs. As a young adult and early twenty-something, I self-sabotaged my desire to connect with other moms I met at my kids' preschool. And this experience continued throughout my son's high school sports participation. I often wanted to get to know the other moms, create friendships, and engage in meaningful conversation, but I talked myself out of it.

And now, as an adult woman in my mid-forties, I see self-sabotage in procrastination, my desire for control, and tendency toward perfectionism. While I'm more apt to go after the big ideas God places in my heart (college and this book), it's the smaller ones I try to avoid. I procrastinate on things like difficult conversations with extended family members. I see my desire for control in the way I self-sabotage my perspective when circumstances feel out of control (if you're parenting young adults, you can probably relate), and I lean into perfectionism when I realize I missed one grammatical error on a PowerPoint presentation. When this happens, I've learned to veer away from perfectionism and into grace. Everyone makes mistakes. One grammatical error doesn't ruin the impact of an insightful presentation.

Why does this happen? Why do we engage in self-sabotage so often? Our brain loves comfort, it enjoys easy, and it won't purposefully sway from routine. When I decide to do something outside my comfort zone, my brain resists, and more than merely resisting, it comes up with all the reasons why I will fail. At our core, most of us have a fear of failure. We don't want to feel embarrassed or uncomfortable. We're only willing to try something new if we have some reason to believe we will succeed. And forget trying to convince yourself with excessive positivity. When our self-talk is negative, it's not hard to envision failure. Our brain only buys into something it can perceive as possible. That's why it's so easy to self-sabotage.

Self-sabotage is a prison cell. It doesn't matter how many people stand outside it cheering us on, imploring us with encouragement, speaking truth and promise; we are the only one who can choose to leave. But the cell is comfortable. We've confined ourselves and locked the door behind us. We've made it our home, decorated the walls with photographic evidence—the reasons why we belong there—and refused to believe anything different. We've convinced ourselves we deserve nothing more than the darkness of that hole. Darkness and disbelief often come from disappointment. Sometimes we've disappointed ourselves, but other times we were disappointed by the people who should've helped us. We've told ourselves no one understands, and no one cares. And although we may not have voiced it directly, we include God in the statement. We convince ourselves everyone else (including God) is responsible for this cell. We believe they have put us there, because it's more comfortable than admitting the truth—we've done this.

And we think we are justified. We've been disappointed by those we thought were authentically invested in our well-being. But instead of admitting our hurt and seeking healing, we build walls around ourselves. We create the prison cell to protect ourselves from future brokenness. And then we say it's their fault—as if our prison cell is their punishment. We tell ourselves they are responsible for restoring our trust, but that's not how it works. We've done this to ourselves. We bought into the lie of self-sabotage. We chose to become its victim. But the good news is since we were the ones who placed ourselves within the cell, we are the ones who can open the door and declare freedom. If we merely open the door and go without embracing the authenticity of our situation, then it won't be long until we're back in that comfortable darkness. And the more often we return to the cell, the longer we stay. I share this awareness with you because I've seen it at work in my life.

Self-sabotage is often the precursor to a victim mentality. Let me clarify. If someone has embraced a victim mentality, they generally feel the whole world is out to get them. They are unwilling to acknowledge any sense of personal responsibility. It's much easier to see this in someone else versus ourselves. Who wants to admit they have allowed self-sabotage to turn them into a victim? I don't, but sometimes it's necessary. I've wasted too many years wanting to do something (tennis lessons, learning a language, and earning a college degree) but telling myself I wasn't smart, capable, or creative. I based this solely on childhood experiences where I wasn't perfect.

Too often, we've convinced ourselves anything less than perfection is a failure. We demand success from ourselves on the first try. And when we can't meet our outrageous expectations, we convince ourselves we shouldn't try anything like that again. But what if we looked at life and the opportunities we face as places of potential? What if we tried the thing we wanted to do, and instead of judging our perceived success or failure, we merely assessed it as a learning experience? How did we grow through it, what would we do the same way next time, and what would we change? Life does not need to be this systematic determination of success or failure. When we embrace opportunities objectively, it keeps our mind in a grace-based space and out of self-sabotage. I spent most of my childhood and early adult years fighting perfectionism. But in recent years, as I've learned to see life not based on success or failure, I'm more apt to go after my dreams.

I (unknowingly) practiced this concept as I entered college. It began with an almost two-week process of asking God questions: *Can I handle this? Will I succeed? What will I study?* I focused on asking questions instead of making negative statements assuming failure. I remained open to His response. As God began to speak, I shifted from uncertainty to excitement. He didn't exactly answer my questions, but I felt a spark of possibility. I began to view it as an opportunity for growth and discovery instead of success or failure. I reminded myself that perfection wasn't the objective—growth was my goal.

My willingness to go after dreams and goals has evolved because I've learned to handle discouragement differently. When we face a place of discouragement, we must process our emotions. That's always important, but we must look at it objectively. If this wasn't my experience, what would I say in response if a friend told me about a similar circumstance and outcome? Does it warrant an equivalent level of discouragement to what I feel about myself? Sometimes I take things too personally and feel them at my core. In these moments, I can take a proactive stance and pursue healing, or I can allow my mindset to embrace negative self-talk, self-sabotage, and, ultimately, a victim mentality.

Instead of choosing to remain in my cell, I can lean into my conversations with God. I can flip through my journal entries where I wrote about my walks on the path with Him or the outcome of questions such as, "God, what do You think of me?" While each tool is beneficial on its own, they provide a multiplied impact when combined. When we are disappointed by others (or ourselves), we feel embarrassed we trusted, and we instinctively want to prevent this experience in the future. Remember, our brain is trying to protect us and keep us comfortable. Self-sabotage partners well with negative self-talk. The two work together to spin a web of lies, and we become trapped. Not only do we fall victim to negative self-talk, but we start to imagine other people's thoughts about us. This is especially true when we've been disappointed by someone. We tell ourselves the other person doesn't care about us or they are too busy to have time to bother with us.

Sometimes our self-sabotage is the result of another person. Often, their well-intentioned comments become daggers in our heart. The phrase, "God won't give you more than you can handle," is NOT in the Bible. It is merely a manufactured statement attempting to move us from brokenness to purpose. While brokenness sometimes leads to purpose, it's not the first step. The danger comes when we agree with that statement, try to tell ourselves we are strong enough to handle the circumstance, and slide further into the cell of discouragement. We know we are not strong enough for *this*. But when a "well-intentioned" individual speaks their catchphrase into our despair, they take advantage of our weakness. Our guard is down, and we trust them. So we nod in agreement while we crumble inside. And in the moment, we don't have the mental fortitude necessary to realize the lunacy of their words, so we take it on as the truth. As a parent, I would never push my child into something hard, painful, and potentially destructive while walking away, yelling over my shoulder, "You can handle it—you're on your own!" This isn't love; it's neglect. God is not a neglectful parent, but many "Christians" have made Him sound that way. Their catchphrases do not serve me well. The statements are not helpful, and they make everything worse because we must process layers of hurt, questioning ourselves, questioning the one who said it, and questioning God. If we take on ill-spoken words, they only further destroy us, and we reinforce the captivity of self-sabotage.

After the death of my daughter, several church members patted me on the shoulder and said, "Well at least she won't suffer, she's in a better place now." Their words stung. Sure, heaven is clearly a better place than earth, and while that may have encompassed the surface level of their statement, it meant something deeper to me. In essence, they were saying it was better for her to be in heaven than on earth, and those words should not be said. I felt myself revert to the confines of my cell, reinforcing their perspective, trying to convince myself their attempt at support was true and I should be happy that she was in heaven instead of in the NICU. And I stayed there for several weeks until I mentioned it to a friend who told me they were wrong. She told me I would have been a wonderful mother and it was okay to feel the pain of this loss. As I processed her encouragement, it was as if she reached into my prison cell, took me by the hand, and lead me out.

When our disappointment is warranted, we benefit from implementing boundaries with the person who hurt us. (I began avoiding those church ladies.) We can keep ourselves out of our prison cell by acknowledging that our emotions were understandable, reminding ourselves we hold the power of belief, and taking responsibility for necessary change. One of the reasons why it's so important to spend time processing our wounds and working through our healing is brokenness breeds pain. Wounded people end up hurting others. It's often not intentional, but we are either working toward healing or allowing the continuation of brokenness. When wounds aren't healed, they become infected, and infections spread. Germs, viruses, and diseases spread until an outside force attacks them. And it's the same for us. Our wounds spread, contaminating other parts of our lives, and impacting the people around us.

If I feel wounded, disappointed, and mistreated by someone, and I don't process the pain, then not only does my attitude change toward that person, but I can also become negative and cynical. The infection spreads. And sometimes, we spread our disease intentionally because it makes us feel better to know someone else feels our pain too. It's not that we think about it consciously or methodically, but it's the reality. We are miserable, and the saying is true—misery loves company.

When our pain spreads to others, we engage in self-sabotage with far-reaching consequences. When we cause brokenness in another person, at some point, we must take responsibility for it. If there's one thing self-sabotage avoids at all costs, it's personal responsibility. Often, the person we infect with our pain has nothing to do with the situation responsible for our brokenness. It's the opposite. We trust them enough to let our guard down, but we do it the wrong way. Instead of embracing vulnerability, we spew our brokenness. And sometimes, we do the same thing with God.

We assume since He allowed this painful experience to happen, He must be okay with it, or He wanted it, but that's not true. Here's what I know about walking out a life impacted by someone else's choices—we all have free will. We make choices. We are not puppets on a string. I do not believe God instigates all our difficulties, but He allows them. It's not because He wants us to become stronger, although strength may be a by-product of our experience. I do not know why He doesn't stop tragedies from occurring, but I believe His plan is redemption. However, when we are reeling from an intentional act that caused us pain, we can end up treating God the way we treat the person who caused our pain. We make sarcastic statements and negative, offhanded comments as if our attitude shows God He was wrong to allow this experience. Even still, God does not push us into a cell, lock the door, and walk away. He does not sabotage our efforts to rebuild our lives, self-belief, or our capacity to see His love. He does not trick us. God doesn't lash out or punish us for expressing our pain, even though we could have done it differently. Instead, He gently speaks to our problem and allows us to take the next step.

One morning, about a month after my husband's death, I said to God, "Why? Why did You make me like this? Why did You cause me to want to be a wife and a mom if I was going to experience such intense loss?" I demanded an answer and held the question as a wall between God and me for several days. And then, I felt Him say, "Marie, you're hurting. I feel your pain." And I knew He meant it. I realized I didn't want an exact answer to my question. Instead, I simply wanted to know He saw my pain. He doesn't force me to apologize or admonish my attitude. His gentleness catches me off guard and reduces my heightened state of emotion.

God is exceedingly patient. He exhibits a level of self-control I cannot comprehend. I'm impatient, but He does not rush me, even when He knows a better way. Here's the reality, when I choose to live within the confines of self-sabotage, I miss out on a relationship with God—I decide not to look for His participation in my life. When I close the door to my cell, I close Him out. But I do not stop Him from trying to break through. He continues to whisper His love. But His whispers go unnoticed most days because my cynicism destroys my ability to hear Him.

And then, one day, everything changes. It's like the first glimmers of sunlight cascading over the horizon in the early morning hours. Darkness is pushed back by the brilliance of a new beginning. God does the same for you and me. His love lights a path out of our darkness. As the light of His love cascades across my captivity, I wake up to the belief that there is more than the limited existence I've created. "God, I want more than this." The whisper of my heart is barely audible. But He hears me, and He's been waiting for these words.

"Yes, Marie, yes. There is so much more. Come out of this cell." He extends His hand toward me, and it feels like when Jesus raised Lazarus from the grave. I was dead inside, and it was my fault, but God is not worried about that right now. I stand up, push against the walls of my confinement, and they fall over. Without my support, the cell can't exist. It was a fictional prison I created. As I take His hand and step out, I realize how self-sabotage has deceived me. I believed others didn't care or didn't want to invest in my life. I thought God wanted me to suffer and this was His best for me. I chose the walls. But they weren't the truth. When I'm disappointed, it's my responsibility to pursue healing, not separation from those I think are at fault (including God).

As God begins to untangle the web of lies from my mind, I see how my cynicism held me captive. I invited it, and the only way to avoid self-sabotage was to stand against it. God has waited for this moment. Calling me out and cheering me on. "There is more to life than this." My longing shifts to confidence and then to my response. "God, I'm sorry I chose self-sabotage instead of You." I reach into my toolbox and pick up the mindset tools that help me work through discouragement. I pop my headset in, crank up my favorite worship station, and head outside for a walk with God. I ask Him to help me see the possibility, to speak the truth about the relationships I can trust and the places where I need to own the restoration process. He does all those things and more. Along the trail, in the back of my neighborhood, He breathes strategy for this day. He gives me purpose and a plan and shows me the next steps. I am not a victim. While I can't control every circumstance, I can control my response. And He's not looking for perfection. Instead, God asks me to live with my heart open.

> *If you came from a place of disappointment where relationships let you down, this is your opportunity to take your pain and stand on it. When we experience pain, it allows us to see the pain in the lives of others.*

In these moments, I go back to the last thing I chose not to do or my most recent place of disappointment. This is my opportunity for a second chance. And if you're tracking with me, this is also your second chance. The thing you told yourself you can't do—you're not strong enough, capable, equipped, whatever it was that excluded you from the task—those reasons are excuses. They are our attempts to save ourselves from failure, but it's not about success or failure. It's simply about doing it. Take a chance on yourself. What's the worst thing that could happen? You'll learn new skills and discover insightful strategies. Even if it doesn't go quite how you planned, you'll find victory because you didn't give up. All you need to do right now is take the first step.

And if you came from a place of disappointment where relationships let you down, this is your opportunity to take your pain and stand on it. When we experience pain, it allows us to see the pain in the lives of others. Someone else needs you to acknowledge the truth of their life. The grief I felt after the loss of my dad was heavy. One day felt excruciating, and not for any specific reason, but just because that's how grief operates. That morning, I asked God to send someone to encourage me. I told Him I didn't need anything fancy; just a simple text would be fine. I needed to know someone saw my pain and cared about me. But when I spoke my request, I felt God respond with a challenge. He asked me to reach out to someone in a similarly difficult season. God asked me to send her a text letting her know I was thinking about her, He cared about her situation, and she was not alone.

For a moment, I was mildly annoyed. I had just asked God to do this very thing for me, but instead of answering my request, He asked me to do it for someone else. However, my annoyance didn't last long. I wanted to be obedient to His invitation, and I knew how much it would have meant to me to receive a similar message. I grabbed my phone, prayed for her, and sent a sincere text. She answered back almost immediately. She said she was having a tough morning and had asked God to give her strength. She felt He had responded to her prayer through my message. When I read her text, I felt I had received more than I had given. I was the one who was encouraged. And I understood why God asked me to text her. He knew not only would she find the strength she desperately needed, but I would also receive the encouragement I desired.

When we partner with God, He can take the smallest act of obedience and transform it into a blessing. God can use us even if our life feels like a train wreck. He's used me in my brokenness, which has become part of my healing journey. There are places of brokenness in your life that offer the same opportunity. You can stand on top of your circumstance and be a beautiful part of someone else's story.

> *When we partner with God, He can take the smallest act of obedience and transform it into a blessing.*

It all starts with one act of obedience. But it doesn't end there. When we link arms with others, it is much harder to find our way back into our cell of self-sabotage. Self-sabotage thrives on isolation. When we cultivate meaningful relationships, they become one of the tools in our toolbox. Not only will they help us stay away from self-sabotage, but they will also become sources of encouragement (which positively impacts our self-talk). Often our closest relationships are formed through the bond of brokenness—someone who can understand our suffering and values our vulnerability. They do not seek to know our pain for "inside information." Instead, they are invested in our lives, want to offer tangible support, and are committed to walking the journey with us. And while there is a vast assortment of tools to use to overcome self-sabotage, we don't need to use them all at once. In this moment, we can pick up the tool closest to us and work on the area that most desperately needs healing.

What does that look like for you? Are you in a cell of self-sabotage? Is God asking you to come out? Or maybe there is a fresh dream inviting you to return to an old (unfinished) goal? Start with the one thing closest to you and allow God to step into that place. He longs for you to hear His voice, heal from the brokenness, and embrace the life He is offering.

Chapter 4
Courage to Dream

The second half of 2012 offered the promise of dreams come true. By September, my dad had finished his chemotherapy and radiation treatments. His oncologist said the (lung cancer) tumor was gone. This news felt like a miracle. He was weak, but we were grateful for the additional time together. I was working through the first draft of my book, *One Light Still Shines*, and our family decided to pursue an international adoption. The horizon line was bright with purpose and promise.

But it was short-lived. There was a storm coming and it wasn't long until the skies were pitch black, the seas were rough, and the promise of dreams come true started to sink beneath the swirling waves. In October, my dad started to feel pain and pressure in his chest. After an assessment and scans, the oncologist confirmed our fears—cancer had returned. There was no cure—the news destroyed me. My dad began another round of chemotherapy, but treatments only offered the potential of a few more months together. He was only sixty-one years old, and I couldn't imagine life without him.

I wish you could have met him. My dad was kind and gentle. He was a thoughtful listener and a deep well of wisdom. He authentically cared about others. We had a close relationship; I talked to him daily and visited almost as frequently. And we weren't close due to his diagnosis. We had always been close. He had an insightful way of seeing the truth, knowing how to serve others in the way they needed most, and a calming presence. Even while he struggled through chemo and radiation, he purposefully looked for moments where he could extend compassion to those who served him or other patients he met. I wasn't surprised when he told me this was his goal for each appointment. It was the quality of his character. When his doctor said there was nothing they could do aside from giving my dad a little more time with his family, he wanted the doctor to know he appreciated everything he had done for him. The world needed my father's influence; my mom needed her husband, I needed my dad, and my kids needed their grandfather. I prayed, begged, and pleaded with God to heal his body.

I did not get the answer I so desperately wanted. On Christmas Eve morning, he had a sudden heart attack and passed away. His doctors attributed his death to the impact of the many rounds of chemotherapy. The reason was not significant. My father was dead, and I felt a deadness inside that was almost indescribable. I raced to my parents' home and sat beside my father's lifeless body on the kitchen floor. The paramedics were still present; their expressions held sorrow and compassion. I stayed with my dad until they took his body away. I drove back home, mentally preparing for the conversation that would follow with my children. I did not want to tell them their grandpa was dead.

When my dad died, my ability to dream died with him. In some ways, I felt God had let me down, and now I was walking another hard road. My dad was a source of strength and stability after the Amish schoolhouse shooting. I didn't know how to navigate tragedy without his steady influence. I didn't know how to help my mom or my siblings, and I felt the pressure to again help my kids find healing. And then there was my healing. How do you ever recover from the loss of your dad?

The context of my prayers focused on my brokenness. "God, I don't want to do any of this." I had lost three grandparents and now my father in the six years since losing my first husband, Charlie. It felt like I was constantly grieving, processing loss, or anticipating the next place of pain. I was emotionally exhausted. Throughout the following weeks and months, I told God I couldn't dream anymore. "Don't ask me to dream; just tell me what You want, and I'll do it." We put our adoption plans on hold. It was hard to write. I could barely see my way through this moment. I could not envision the beautiful future which seemed almost tangible a few months earlier. I certainly did not want to dream. The process of dreaming was risky. There were no guarantees the things I envisioned would become a reality. In that season, dreaming seemed only to bring disappointment.

I thought God was okay with my stance because He didn't pressure me. For months I lived in obedience, saying yes to His requests but refusing to dream. And then, one morning, when I muttered my usual prayer, "Just tell me what You want me to do today," I felt Him ask me to dream. Almost instantaneously, I said no. "God, I'm not dreaming. Dreaming brings disappointment, and I cannot endure more of it." My brokenness met God's grace. There was a tinge of arrogance in my refusal to dream. As if I was saying I was not dreaming because God had disappointed me. God could've called me out, challenged my attitude, and corrected my perspective, but He let it go. He knew I needed love and healing more than discipline.

"Marie, it's all about your expectations." And with one simple sentence, He changed me. I realized that instead of holding on to the expectancy of God showing up as I pursued these dreams, I was holding on to the expectation of a clearly defined outcome. My disappointment was the result of unmet expectations. As I began to dream with God, I anticipated the outcome or result my mind perceived as logical. However, my life doesn't take a logical path. When I dreamt about my dad overcoming cancer, I held fast to the manifestation of physical healing. When I dreamt about the process of writing a book, I envisioned myself holding the final copy instead of endless writing and rewriting. Regardless of the dream, my perceived result was always a "happy ending."

Whenever God birthed a new dream, I immediately envisioned the ending. It was almost instinctual, but it led to negative self-talk and self-sabotage. Thoughts like, *Nothing ever works out for me* and *Why can't my life be easy like everyone else's?* assaulted my mind. If left unchecked, these thoughts turn to insecurity, jealousy, and feelings of worthlessness. Have you ever felt God didn't love you as much as someone else because their life looked easier or thought He was constantly setting you up for failure because nothing ever worked out for you? We've probably all felt that way at least once.

My life contains hardship and dreams that did not come true the way I envisioned. But I don't believe it is because God doesn't love me or loves me less than someone else. Here's what I know, God loves me enough to step into my circumstance and walk with me. He met me in the first moments as the Amish schoolhouse shooting unfolded. God gave me strength that was not my own. On October 2, 2006, I chose to believe God is everything He promised—healer, helper, strength, hope, my redemption, and that, despite this event, He would rescue me. I was a stay-at-home mom with three children. My husband murdered five innocent girls and wounded five more before taking his life. If I created a definition of my future based on these circumstances, an expectation of anything good would not exist.

This one experience was vastly different than all others. In this moment, I did not project an expected outcome. I did not envision my "happy ending." I couldn't. There was no way for me to take the broken pieces of my life and figure out how to reassemble them. While I believed God would bring healing, hope, and restoration, I did not tie them to a specific plan for my future. And it made all the difference. God continued to exceed my hope throughout the weeks, months, and years following the shooting. Instead of placing my expectations on Him, I put my hope in Him.

But as the years passed, I lost that perspective. It slipped through my fingers, and I didn't even realize it was gone. I focused on my expectations instead of hope. But our dreams hinge on hope. When I place my hope in God, He does more than I could imagine. When I put my hope in expectations, I am constantly disappointed because circumstances won't match my demands. Expectations are demands, and when I create expectations of my future, I am, in essence, demanding God follow my plans.

I have learned I am not in control. Sometimes it's hard for me to admit the truth. I like the illusion of control (thank you, Oogway from *Kung Fu Panda*). I want to grab hold of the belief that I control circumstances, but the harder I fight to take control, the more frustrated I become. And I will never win. I do not control the circumstance of my life, I do not control other people, and I do not control God. My control lies in my response and where I place my hope.

If I am going to partner with God, embrace His dream for my life, and work with Him, I must relinquish control and embrace the hope He offers. I must dream *with* Him, one step at a time, envisioning all parts of the process as they arise, and not skip from the beginning straight to the end. And it is hard for me. I don't want to think about all the work it will take to fulfill a dream. I want to go from the emotional high of the moment God released a dream in my heart directly to the magnificent end I've envisioned. But when I focus on the end point, I miss all the adventures along the way, and these adventures ultimately lead to the ending. Without the middle portion, I'd never arrive at the destination. Sometimes the dream changes in the middle because, by the midpoint, I've changed. By the time I reach any ending, I'm not the person I was initially. I learn and grow. Sometimes this directly relates to me, and other times it is within the context of the project. But knowing this helps me understand why an immediate jump from start to finish results in disappointment. I must embrace the adventure, welcome opportunities for growth, and allow the path to twist and turn from beginning to end. It's easy for me to become so fixated on efficiency—getting from the starting line to the finish line as quickly as possible, that I forget how much I love adventure.

My realization brings deeper understanding; when I'm captivated by the ending, I become task-oriented, constantly focused on activities that propel me closer to *my* goal. But this isn't how God asks me to approach dreaming with *Him*. Dreaming with God is not task-based; it's an adventure. It offers the opportunity to get to know Him in a new or more profound way. It provides the ability to find strengths inside of me I didn't know existed. We are partnering *with* God; He has created this adventure with us in mind. He knows our likes and dislikes, where we need to challenge ourselves, and incorporates special moments of connection. When we look at the concept of dreaming with God as an unforgettable adventure we take *with* Him, it changes the entire story.

Let's look at it this way. Imagine I planned a special day with one of my kids. We'd go to breakfast at his favorite creperie, followed by shopping, then lunch from his favorite Chinese restaurant (hello, orange chicken), watch a new Marvel movie, then test-drive his dream car just for fun, and finally, dinner at the best spot to grab wings! I couldn't wait to watch his eyes light up as we began every activity. I wanted him to know how much I loved him. It would be a day filled with unforgettable memories. I decided to keep it a secret, so I only shared our starting time and where we were going for dinner. However, throughout every experience, all he could talk about was a dozen wings he would eat. While he probably enjoyed breakfast, shopping, lunch, the movie, and browsing cars, he didn't seem to appreciate any of it. He only thought about the ending. If this happened, I would feel frustrated by the time and money I spent making the whole day special. Honestly, I wouldn't care about dinner at his favorite restaurant; instead, I would probably resent it.

As much as I wouldn't want to experience this scenario, the truth is I do this to God. When He asks me to partner with Him on a dream, and I immediately jump to the ending, I ignore all the other moments spent with Him—moments He planned for me along the way. I miss the surprises, I don't (wholeheartedly) participate in the adventure, and undoubtedly disappoint God. And that's why I become disappointed—because I'm impatient. My impatience hurts the One who has carried, redeemed, strengthened, and healed me. This realization is painful. Typing it out makes me pause. I would have given up on myself a long time ago. I would not have extended additional opportunities to dream together. I would have moved on to someone else, but God has not given up on me. And He hasn't given up on you, either.

> *I must stop jumping to conclusions. I cannot begin unfolding a dream with God based on the perspective that I already know the ending.*

It doesn't matter how impatient we've been, how frequently we've missed the point, or how often our preconceived ending has consumed us; God offers another opportunity. And now that I understand where (and why) I miss the point of dreaming, I do not want to miss it again. Now, when God extends the opportunity to partner with Him, I want to participate in the entire adventure. I don't want the abbreviated version. I want every twist and turn, each surprise, and every special moment planned just for me. I want to enjoy it *with* Him.

However, to do that, I must stop jumping to conclusions. I cannot begin unfolding a dream with God based on the perspective that I already know the ending. And this is hard. I am not arrogant and self-absorbed. I willingly acknowledge I don't understand everything. It comes from a well-intentioned place inside me. I am a quick thinker and good at problem-solving, so it's almost instinctive for me to look at a plan from a task-based mindset. And in any other setting, this approach is appropriate. But God doesn't need me to take charge. He asks me to participate, and there is room for my ideas at His table. God invites me to invest in our project, but I get to do it with Him—not on my own.

A sense of vulnerability exists when we partner with someone else. We must relinquish sole control (you already know that's not my strength) and lean into the partnership. I'm not fond of group projects. Throughout my entire school experience (including my recent college studies), group projects generally result in me doing a large portion of the work. And yes, it's my fault because I have very high standards. I'm not going to turn in something that wasn't my best effort, so if I can't trust someone else to work at a level equal to my expectations, I take over.

But I diminish God's authority, creativity, and adventure when I try to take over. I can trust Him. He is trustworthy. God is not the problem; I am. From the moment He begins to reveal a plan, I'm like the race car driver, waiting to step on the gas and shift through gears and opponents as I work my way to the finish line. I want to win and prove I'm exceptional. But I don't need to prove anything to God. This dream is not a race. He's not asking me to smash the accelerator to the floor. Instead, He wants me to slow down and enjoy the adventure, but slow is hard; fast is easy.

Dreaming with God is not about racing down the highway 5–10 mph over the speed limit, constantly checking the GPS for a faster route. It's taking the back roads, stopping at the farm stands to grab some produce, and pulling off at the scenic overlook to take pictures. It means I enjoy the beauty around me instead of keeping my eyes glued to the road ahead. It's Lightning McQueen and Miss Sally driving on Route 66—taking in the vistas, being changed by the surroundings, and etching each moment in your heart/mind forever.

While dreaming with God, I must remind myself to trust Him. I can look back at our relationship and see where He met me. I must step back into the surprises He planned just for me and the beautiful outcomes I wouldn't have imagined. It's in those places I remember why I need to relinquish control. It always ends better than I could imagine. What does it look like to partner with God this way? Considering my weaknesses, it's this: I let God lead.

> But God doesn't need me to take charge. He asks me to participate, and there is room for my ideas at His table. God invites me to invest in our project, but I get to do it with Him—not on my own.

I talk with Him: "God, thank You for the opportunity to partner with You on this dream. I'm excited about what You have in store, and I can't wait to watch the adventure unfold. God, help me to capture every moment the way You intend. I don't want to miss anything. If I'm moving too fast, slow me down. If I try to take control, stop me. Gently redirect me when I get in the way. I yield my heart, will, and desires to Your plan."

And then, in that moment and every one after, I ask Him what I should focus on during this day. Sometimes He draws me to a task, but often it's a theme. While writing this book, God has encouraged me to focus on "freely and lightly" from Matthew 11:28–30 (*The Message*). "Are you tired? Worn out? Burned out on religion? Come to me. Get away with me and you'll recover your life. I'll show you how to take a real rest. Walk with me and work with me—watch how I do it. Learn the unforced rhythms of grace. I won't lay anything heavy or ill-fitting on you. Keep company with me and you'll learn to live freely and lightly."

God knows I don't often need reminders to get to work. I'm an overachiever. But I need the reminder to slow down, to take the self-imposed weight off my shoulders—walk, work, and rest His way. When I let God lead and stay in a place defined by Matthew 11:28–30, it reduces (or eliminates) my tendency to get burned out or overwhelmed. I am purposefully admitting I am not in control. I'm authentically committed to His process. It's not that I'm saying He's in control "just to make it sound good"; I mean it. I know the starting point, but I have no idea where we're going or how we will get there. I can trust God will reveal each step exactly when I need to see it. And when that happens, it becomes one of the vistas which takes my breath away.

It's okay if this process sounds scary or uncomfortable; it's also okay if you don't get it right 100 percent of the time. There are still times when I try to head toward the highway, prepared to drive as fast as possible on the way to my perceived destination. But God knows my heart—I want Him to redirect me, and He does. Just as He meets me in my weakness and helps me find His way, He will do the same for you, even if you're starting from a deficit. Maybe you're in the same place I was a few years ago; you don't want to dream because you're afraid you'll face additional disappointment. God will meet you there too. Freely and lightly, that's all He wants for you. Let Him lead.

Chapter 5
Cue the Celebration

It's time to talk about celebrating. It's not just because you've worked through the previous chapters on mindset, negative self-talk, self-sabotage, and embracing the courage to dream. I mean, your progress is absolutely a reason to celebrate. But we deserve to celebrate more than just our hard work. When I've viewed celebration as something I had to earn based on the accomplishment of tasks, I've experienced less joy, more stress, and higher levels of procrastination. When celebration only occurs after a milestone, it reinforces the belief that we earn it through achievements. The more we tell ourselves we must earn the celebration, the less we feel like we deserve to celebrate because we easily identify all the reasons we have not earned it. We didn't . . .

- Finish all the items on our to-do list
- Stick to our diet
- Drink enough water
- Spend enough time with God
- Have enough patience

It's not so much about the specifics of why we don't qualify for a celebration, instead, it becomes a foundational belief that we aren't worth celebrating.

When was the last time you celebrated yourself? If your answer is, "I can't remember" or "Never," we need to dig up and re-lay your foundation. The art of celebrating ourselves (and it is an art) directly correlates to our mindset and specifically negative self-talk and self-sabotage. When we reinforce our value through celebration, we create a positive truth regarding our self-worth. You may be thinking, *Well, what is worth celebrating?* Everything—all the small wins. And as we begin to embrace this concept, we must celebrate it all. For example, if executing daily habits is a struggle, and you made it to work on time—celebrate! You often grab takeout but packed your lunch or made dinner—celebrate! You usually forget to switch the laundry but this time you put it in the washer and switched it to the dryer all on the same day—celebrate! You thought about texting a family member or friend a note of encouragement, and you did it—celebrate! Maybe you think I'm making it too easy, but here's the thing, for most of us, celebrating ourselves is a new concept. It's one we struggle with and generally avoid. To become comfortable with celebration and find value in who we are, we often must start with daily tasks connected to a larger goal. It's a little like potty training a toddler. You initially give them an M&M just because they sat on the toilet. You're not expecting them to do anything; you simply reward them for the small step. You're training them to associate using the bathroom with something good. After they've sat on the potty a few times, you up the stakes; they must pee in the potty to receive their reward. We may not always celebrate that we made it to work on time, remembered to switch the laundry from the washer to the dryer, or sent an encouraging text message, but in the beginning, we are training our brains to identify follow-through.

Begin by identifying the things that almost seem too easy for one week. Then the following week, raise the stakes and demand more of yourself. By focusing on the prior week's successes, you'll have a truth-based foundation upon which to build. During week one, if you celebrated getting up on time each day, add three mornings of exercise in week two. If you don't like exercising, start with a small amount of time (15–20 minutes), and choose an enjoyable activity. You'll have the capacity to believe you can exercise for fifteen minutes three times a week because you have already proven to yourself that you can get up on time. Remember to celebrate at the end of the week.

> The art of celebrating ourselves (and it is an art) directly correlates to our mindset and specifically negative self-talk and self-sabotage. When we reinforce our value through celebration, we create a positive truth regarding our self-worth.

What kind of celebration is meaningful to you? Many online assessments promise to help you determine motivating forces, and one of my favorites is the Love Languages Quiz. This quiz will enable you to understand which of the five love languages best corresponds to you. While Dr. Gary Chapman developed the concept of the Five Love Languages for the benefit of person-to-person relationships, I believe it also applies to our relationship with ourselves. In case you're unfamiliar, the Five Love Languages, are acts of service, receiving gifts, quality time, words of affirmation, and physical touch. Sometimes it's hard to determine a meaningful way to celebrate. Using my love language helps me avoid the frustration of trying to figure it out. Gifts are my dominant love language. It doesn't mean I take myself shopping for every celebration, but if that works for you, do it! Sometimes it means a coffee out, new lipstick, or pair of chandelier earrings. But other times I gift myself the time necessary to make (and enjoy) an espresso at home, a ten-minute power nap, or a couple hours to organize my closet. If your love language is quality time, celebrate by planning lunch with a friend or a coffee date with your spouse. If your love language is acts of service or physical touch, you'll have to get creative and involve someone else. For physical touch, if your significant other is willing, ask them for a foot or shoulder rub. If acts of service feel like a treat to you, ask someone in your household to do a chore you despise, or treat yourself to a house cleaning service.

If using your love language doesn't feel like a good fit, consider the way you enjoy celebrating someone else. Generally, our first inclination is to take care of others in the way that is most meaningful for us. It may feel hard to celebrate yourself initially because you're building a new skill. When we try something new, the first few attempts often feel challenging, but each subsequent time gets easier. The more often we celebrate ourselves, the more we start to identify those things that are most meaningful. Give yourself grace and time to figure it out. Above all, ask God to help you understand the way He celebrates you. It's okay to ask Him for the celebration. I'll be honest; there are days I've asked Him for a gift. There are moments when we need encouragement, the reminder He sees us and our lives matter.

One of the ways he shows up in my life, when I ask for a gift, is through feathers. In May 2020, my husband and I celebrated our 13th anniversary. For the past few years, we have always planned a weekend away near our anniversary—as a blended family, our relationship exists around our kids. We've only known each other as parenting spouses, so setting aside time to focus on being a couple is essential. That year, I was a little sad about the circumstances; we hadn't even been out on a date since early March due to the various viral restrictions. We tried to create intentional moments together, but it was more difficult than usual. Our time consisted of walks in the evenings when the weather was nice. I knew that in the grand scheme of things, I shouldn't complain.

We were healthy, our family was fine, and our relationship was solid. Yet, my heart longed for the celebration we had planned months before and time away together.

A few weeks before our anniversary, I told my husband I wanted to find a black shirt with white polka dots. It was completely random. I don't know why I was so set on it; except I had looked for one (unsuccessfully) over the past three years. My husband made it his secret mission to surprise me with this shirt. He gave it to me a few days before our anniversary—his tangible love touched my heart.

However, the shirt was not the biggest surprise in store for us. We went for our nightly walk on our anniversary. As we journeyed along the wooded path near our house, we spotted a feather lying on the ground. It was black with white polka dots! When I stopped to pick it up, I realized there were two feathers, one lying on top of the other! God showed up majestically with an anniversary gift I won't ever forget. He heard the cry of my heart and answered with a stunning level of tenderness and compassion.

I don't think God is offended when we ask. I also don't think He needs us to ask—He knows every thought. But I need to say it so I'm looking for, and aware of, His response. This is another place of relationship I view through the lens of parenthood. If one of my kids is struggling, I want to understand what's happening in their world. However, there are days when I can tell they are struggling, but I don't know why, or they don't want to talk about it. When this happens, I make an extra effort to interact with them in a way that's meaningful. My kids have taken the Love Languages Quiz, which gives me insight into the best strategy to show them I care.

But there are times I miss it. In the busyness of life, I can mistake quietness for focus instead of realizing they are struggling with a situation. Before they could drive, they would often ask to go somewhere, which offered a break from whatever they were processing. When they asked if I would take them to McDonald's or Sonic, I wasn't annoyed. Instead, I was grateful they asked. They asked and I responded. My response built trust and reinforced the positive attributes of our relationship. The same thing happens when we ask God for the type of interaction we need from Him.

When I ask God for a gift, I'm not explicitly asking Him to drop a package (or a feather) by my door. I'm asking Him to meet me in such a way that I know it's an answer to my prayer. It may not always come as I envisioned, but He shows up. I remind myself that when I ask, God responds. It builds my relationship with Him and helps me to trust Him in the future. Celebration is not optional and won't happen unless we plan for it. It may sound counterintuitive, but scheduling moments of celebration is necessary. Without planning, we will continue to put it off, feel like we haven't earned it, or avoid it. We are adept at putting others first and assuming we can focus on ourselves when we accomplish everything else. If we don't purposefully schedule celebration, it will fall into this category.

I call it Cinderella Syndrome. She was constantly taking care of the household chores and the demands of her stepfamily while reassuring herself she would have time to sew her ballgown later. As my husband tells our kids, "Later never comes." There is always something else to do. We have a list, a mile long, of tasks we must accomplish, and often these center around other people. We tell ourselves if we finish it all, we can move on to the things we want to do for ourselves. We use this list of personally focused items as our celebration, and while the concept is fine, the execution is a problem. We won't ever finish everything. There will always be someone or something else vying for our attention. The only way we can break through is to schedule our celebration.

Pick one day each week and give yourself at least twenty to thirty minutes to inventory and celebrate your success. Write down all the small wins for the week. Better yet, write them down during the week as they happen. Review your list and remind yourself of all the places where you've taken action in your life. Then celebrate with the reward you planned. Maybe you enjoy window-shopping on Amazon, giving yourself fifteen minutes to use your electronic back massager, or researching robot vacuum cleaners. (If your love language is acts of service, look for something that can provide a shortcut or eliminate one of your tasks—like vacuuming!) Then plan to pick up where you left off the following week.

One of the things I often hear from my coaching clients is they struggle to find joy in their lives. Sure, they are happy at certain moments of the day, but there's no overall sense of joy. My first question in response to this comment is, what activities are meaningful or enjoyable for you? They usually say things like reading on my porch, going on a run with my dog, catching up with a friend, taking a cooking class, cleaning out my closet, or having time alone in my house. The next thing I ask is how often they engage in these activities. Most of the time, they say they aren't pursuing any of them because they are too busy. Due to work, home, and family demands, there's not enough time to take a break. When we experience this type of situation, we often become resentful of others (it's happened to me). We feel annoyed because our spouse seems to have so much free time while we struggle to get everything done. We become jealous while scrolling through social media because a friend is always going somewhere, but we can't even get five minutes to ourselves. We see our kids sitting around on their phones, and we start muttering under our breath that they should be helping with more household chores. Our negative self-talk loves conversations like these.

I realize our family members won't always say yes when we ask them to participate in household tasks. Instead, we must ask for help, be willing to let the chores go, and create opportunities to take time out from everyday life. Similarly, if you're feeling overworked, your boss may not care to listen to your (legitimate) reasons why your workload is too much. However, we are worth squeezing 20–30 minutes of joy-producing time into our day. If you're giving up your lunch break to increase efficiency or taking work home at night or on the weekend, stop. If you continually focus on one household task after another—take a break. Engaging in life-giving activities isn't optional; it's necessary. You will gain a more positive outlook and feel an increase in creativity, not to mention it will lower your stress level, when you give yourself some time each day. All those T-shirts with "hustle harder" sayings are wrong. Hustling harder doesn't increase satisfaction; instead, it leads us down the path of increased frustration. We don't need to work harder, we need to cultivate moments of joy.

And if it's been so long since you did anything for yourself that you don't even know where to start, I understand. But it's no reason to avoid it. If you're having trouble finding activities that sound like fun, and one more decision feels exhausting, take a nap. Rest for fifteen or twenty minutes. You don't have to sleep; play some relaxing music while you close your eyes. Don't think about any responsibilities; concentrate on breathing deeply. If you need to focus your mind on something, recite Scripture, a poem, or pray. Sometimes we are so physically and mentally exhausted we can't make one more decision. When this happens, rest is best. Think about previous times when you had a higher level of joy. What were some activities you engaged in frequently? Did you love attending a Zumba class with your friends? Did you visit art museums on the weekend and sketch your favorite piece? Maybe you challenged yourself to create a Pinterest-worthy craft or recipe. Try picking up a hobby you enjoyed months or years ago.

A few years ago, I found myself in this same place. I wasn't engaging in joy-producing activities. I felt like I served everyone else and never had time for myself. I remember texting my husband one morning because I finally had two free hours I could devote to myself, but I felt frustrated because I couldn't think of anything to do. The frustration multiplied as I felt the minute tick by, wasted on frantic soul-searching. I asked Dan what I should do, and he reminded me I hadn't played the piano in years. His suggestion was perfect. I love playing the piano when no one is home, and I can create my own melodies without anyone else listening. I don't remember the specific melody I played that day, but it revived my weariness. That day became a catalyst. I found myself sitting at the piano often, even when I only had ten minutes of free time. It sparked creativity and became my form of personal celebration. My piano became a cherished friend with whom I had deep and meaningful conversations, without ever saying a word.

There are times when circumstance turns up the intensity in our lives. During those seasons, we must also increase time spent on joy-inducing activities. I understand it's harder to feel like we have the mental and physical energy necessary to do these things, but our lives depend on it. It feels more productive to work harder, push the pain aside, and "put on our big girl panties," but this mindset only leads to further exhaustion. When we (physically and mentally) start to enter the danger zone, we can choose to ignore the signs. We lack motivation, feel disinterested in the things we used to enjoy, don't take care of ourselves the way we used to, and everything feels more complicated. These are signals something is wrong, and as much as we don't feel like it, we must correct our course immediately.

If we choose to ignore the signs, we head into the zone known as burnout. Think about it like a bank account. If your expenses exceed your income, but you have a little cushion, you can manage this pace for a while—you wait longer to pay bills, put some things on a credit card, and exhaust your savings. But you can't sustain it permanently. It eventually catches up with you. The cushion is gone, you've maxed out the credit cards, and there's no room in your budget for additional expenses. If you can't reduce costs or increase income, your account slides into a negative balance. And the further you go into negative territory, the harder it is to climb out. Burnout works the same way. At first, it seems like you can handle it. You tell yourself you can dig deep and manage the stress. You continue to say yes to additional responsibilities, while reducing down-time, even though you desperately want to say no.

You don't know how to stop this cycle. Everyone thinks you're capable, so they keep piling more work on your shoulders. The load is exhausting. You stop exercising because you're too tired, and you're sleeping fewer hours each night. It's hard to fall asleep, and when you finally manage to drift off, you're awakened a few hours later by a racing heartbeat. The anxiety and stress are causing tightness in your chest. You want to scream and run away, but that would cause more work, so you stay. You reach for a sugar fix or a caffeinated beverage mid-afternoon because you don't have enough energy to make it through the day. Instead of counting the ounces of water you're consuming, you try to laugh it off when you realize all you are drinking is caffeine to stay energized and then alcohol to take the edge off. You're drowning, and no one notices.

If you're reading this and feel a lightbulb turn on, there's no shame in recognizing burnout; and the good news is you can recover from it. During the recovery process, prioritize sleep, proper nutrition, and water. Spend time with people who offer a supportive relationship. Set healthy boundaries, especially where you've felt resentful for the load piled on your shoulders. Engage in some form of physical movement each day—whether you enjoy walks, yoga, weightlifting, or dance, find a way to stay active. And look for opportunities to reduce your stress level. Guided meditation, art and mindfulness, deep breathing, and prayer are a few of my favorites. And at any point when we recognize we need to strengthen how we approach our mental well-being, it's always appropriate to ask for help. There are well-trained mental health professionals who can help you. If you're unsure where to start, check out the resources on www.psychologytoday.com. You can search for a counselor in your area, read their bio, and discover services offered.

Sometimes it is difficult to celebrate; during those seasons, we must evaluate the cause and determine where we can create positive change. In this place, it's still about small steps. If you realize you're suffering from burnout, celebrate your self-awareness. Celebrate the changes you're making which will lead to a more positive life experience. You deserve to feel joy again. We all have wounds that need healing. Maybe they aren't as deep as burnout, but they exist. Healing is worth celebrating. You, your life, and the journey you're on are worth celebrating.

Chapter 6
Introductions

It's time for me to officially introduce you to someone whose love and care have permeated my life and the previous chapters. I want to give you the opportunity to know Him and build your own relationship. And maybe you're wondering why it's taken six chapters to get to this point. Let me explain. I did not place this introduction at the start of our conversation because I didn't want to go there first. I didn't want to take you straight to the destination, so instead, I've taken you on a scenic drive. It's given you the opportunity to hear my backstory and perspectives before I made this introduction.

But now, it's time. We need to talk about God. And if mentioning His name causes you to feel wary of all that comes next, please don't stop reading. Many people have misrepresented Him. Churches and religious institutions spew doctrine, attitudes, and false beliefs far from His ideas. If you have been mistreated by those who proclaim to follow Him, please know they didn't align their motives with His heart. I understand. I've experienced brokenness at the hands of those who said they were followers of Jesus. At some points in my life, the church has wounded and abandoned me. If I based my relationship with God on those who say they represent Him, I would have run away from Him.

But I won't allow fallible people or false doctrine to keep me away from the one who authentically loves me. And I don't want them to become the barricade that stands between you and your Father.

You deserve a relationship with Him. Set the institution of religion aside and come with me as I introduce you to Him. Allow this space to be inhabited by you and God alone, free from aspects of control, abandonment, manipulation, and fear. I'm here with you. Trust me as I walk with you. It's a place of deeper connection. If you already know God, there is more for you to discover. As much as we could ever know, we have only begun to understand His deep love and genuine care. He is real. He's not a fable in a storybook, but He's also not the guarantee of "happily ever after."

If you have been mistreated by those who proclaim to follow Him, please know they didn't align their motives with His heart.

He has existed for all time, knows your name, and authentically invests Himself in every moment of your life. God brought you here. What are the chances you and I would connect? Let's trace the story backward from the moment when you picked up this book. How did it happen? It was not a coincidence—it was God.

He has waited for the day when you would enter the same room as He and not feel afraid. He has one desire—to love you. It is the purest form of love you could ever hope to experience. Love—not for the sake of reciprocation but love simply for love's sake. He wants this relationship more than you could ever know. He wants you to cultivate connection with Him—morning walks, coffee on the porch, painting, writing, and expressing the creativity He placed inside you. He longs for you to live from a place where you authentically believe and search for evidence of His presence in your life. He is all around you, whispering through the flowers, and smiling through the beam of sunshine that falls upon your face. He's in the small moments that take your breath away, the victories that deserve a celebration, and He steadies you when the ground shakes.

Whether you feel uncertain you're ready or you can't wait to know Him more, your next step is the same. Invite Him into this day. Don't skip ahead five steps down the road and try to imagine everything that will happen from today forward. Embrace the present moment, ask Him to show you the places He inhabited throughout your past, and look with expectancy at the adventures you'll have together in the future.

We don't have to walk this road alone, and you don't have to take one more step by yourself. The truth is, God has walked with you even when you didn't know He was there. Sometimes we try so hard to convince ourselves we are strong enough that it is difficult to take off the mask and embrace the authentic version of ourselves. We've had to do so many things alone, even when we didn't want to; it's easier to pretend that we are capable. Admitting weakness feels vulnerable.

But vulnerability is the point. God is not asking us to be strong. He's not "doing this to make you stronger." He is not looking at you, thinking you look weak and need to work out. Your circumstances are not His idea of a supernatural gym membership. Yes, often, we develop strength through our trials (they change us), but strength is not God's primary goal. So if it feels hard to allow Him into your heart because you're frustrated by this season, tell Him. If you can fill in this sentence, talk to Him about it. "It's hard for me to build a relationship with God because _____." So many lines "Christians" use are not in the Bible, and they're not God's heart. Here are a few of my least favorites:

- God gives His most challenging battles to His strongest soldiers.
- God won't give us more than we can handle.

- Everything happens for a reason.
- Pray harder.

If you're emotionally exhausted, tired of fighting, and annoyed with people who give meaningless commentary on your life, tell God. He's not going to become frustrated by your honesty. He welcomes it. Authentic connections happen through transparency. Think about your best friend; they are the person you can tell anything. You don't have to hold back your deepest thoughts, and they won't say you're crazy. They know when to give advice and when to listen. God is the same, and so much more. While He knows our faults and flaws, He doesn't structure conversations to remind us of them. God's not that annoying kid from junior high who loved to remind you He was smarter than you. He listens, and He understands. He is not disappointed in you, you haven't gotten too far away from Him, and He will never leave you. If you've never had the opportunity to build a relationship with Him or need a fresh start, it can happen through a simple conversation. You can say these words aloud or within your mind. Either way, He will hear and respond.

"Jesus, I want to get to know You. This concept of relationship is new for me, but I want to learn how to trust You. I want to see You at work in my life and receive Your invitation to experience the adventure You have in store for me. I know I'm not perfect. I have made mistakes. I've doubted myself. But I want more. I want more than what I see right now. God, I welcome You into my life. Come and make Your home within my heart. Speak to me. Lead me. Love me. I will walk with You forever."

You might feel the emotion of your prayer, or you might not feel anything. If you experience a physical sensation (some people feel warmth or tingling), write it down so you remember this moment. If you don't feel anything though, that's okay too. Write down the date and time so you can look back in the coming weeks and remember this catalyst. You have changed the trajectory of your life.

Relationship with God isn't all about emotion. Yes, I sometimes feel emotion, it hits a deep place in my heart, and I can't let go of it. But I'm not always going to feel that same heightened emotion every time I think about the words He speaks, His presence, or His love for me. I experienced this when God spoke to me about adoption. Dan and I married in May 2007, and at the time, our five children ranged in age from two to sixteen years old. Life was chaotic and wonderful. We were figuring out the process of creating our family. Often (well-meaning) people would ask when we were planning to have a baby. I was twenty-nine, and Dan was forty, so the thought of a biological child wasn't out of the question. However, even though I love babies, I knew this wasn't part of God's plan for our family. My kids had been through a traumatic loss plus the new marriage, and I didn't want to bring additional stress and uncertainty to them in the form of a child shared by Dan and me. Our children needed time to adjust and feel confident within our family.

However, about six months into our marriage, I felt God begin to speak to me about adoption. I remembered how I felt after my children lost their father. I became acutely aware that while my kids had undergone a severe loss, many children worldwide don't have the blessing of even one parent. At the time, I tucked the thought away. But God brought it out eight months later in our sixth month of marriage. I casually asked Dan one morning what he thought about adoption. He said, "Marie, we have five children—count them, five! We have the opportunity for five simultaneous crises on any given day." And he was right. But I felt God speak adoption in a way that pulsed through my body—I knew it was God.

While I'm not always the most patient person, I did not want Dan to say yes to adoption because I refused to stop asking. I can be persuasive when I am passionate about a topic, and I knew it was wrong to convince him adoption was the next step for our family. I began to pray God would speak to Dan the same way He had spoken to me. Every few months, I would ask Dan, "What's God speaking to your heart about adoption?" This phrase sounded better than asking what he was thinking and carried the context of my intention through the question. I only wanted Dan to meet me in the middle of this conversation if it was something God had stirred.

I believed one day Dan would say yes, and I was ready. I had prayed and waited five years. One morning when I asked that question again, Dan replied, "You know, God *has* been speaking to my heart about adoption." I told him I was excited to hear him say those words and said there was an excellent adoption agency in our community. The office was located less than a mile from where he worked, and they had an informational meeting scheduled the following week. I asked if I should sign us up. He looked a little stunned; it was the infamous "deer-in-headlights" look. He didn't know I was doing my research in addition to praying and waiting.

Throughout those five years, there were many times I did not feel emotion or passion for adoption. Since Dan was not in agreement, I couldn't talk to him about my thoughts or dreams. I'm sure he would have listened, but it was unfair to continue talking about a process he wasn't ready to begin. However, I knew God had placed it on my heart for a purpose, and I wasn't going to let it go. I prayed and waited, and God worked even when I had no idea it was happening. And just as God continued to work in my life and within my family while I was unaware, He does the same in you.

He's been working in your life to bring you to this exact moment when you and I would share this conversation. And He will continue to work in your life from this day forward. There will be times when you will sense His presence; you might see Him in the people around you, experience His love in a random act of kindness, or feel a word of encouragement He deposited in your heart. However, there may also be times when you may feel disconnected from Him. You may struggle to get back to a place of vibrant relationship and wonder what you've done to cause this separation. In both experiences, God remains invested in our lives. Many people offer explanations for why they experience these quiet times. You can find endless answers or strategies in books, podcasts, and other online resources. They could help you overcome a period of silence. I will share my experiences too, but I'm just one person. Any strategy you read is the experience of one individual. We are all unique. Something that makes sense or works well for me (or someone else) may not work for you.

When I've experienced periods where God seems distant or quiet, I've learned to lean into it. I ask questions and reflect because the process works for me. I begin this way, "Have I failed to follow through on something God and I talked about?" And then I wait, allowing an opportunity for God to bring a conversation to mind. If I remember something I missed, I do it right away. I've learned if I forget or attempt to avoid a task or conversation He placed on my heart, I've effectively hit the "pause" button on our relationship. But sometimes, it has nothing to do with forgetting or avoiding an assignment. In those moments, I try to let go of all I think I know about my relationship with God. I approach it as a new adventure.

God speaks in a variety of ways. It's not that He gets bored with one communication style, and I can't tell you exactly why He changes His methods, but He does. When I feel Him shift away from our predictable type of communication, I remind myself it's not necessarily because I've done something wrong. It's not that I can't hear Him. But I must open my heart, find a new rhythm, and allow Him to lead this adventure. Often, it's difficult because

I don't want to slow down and take the time necessary to figure Him out. I don't want to have to invest in looking for God in a new way. I want to slide into the path I know because it's easier.

I know how to find Him there. Sometimes my actions (or inactivity) tell Him I don't want to pursue a relationship with Him. I want Him to do the work, not me. But this isn't the way relationship works. Deep, meaningful relationships include an equal investment. Knowing these things doesn't always motivate me to do them. I am human. I get tired, and honestly, sometimes, I'm lazy. God won't force me to pursue our relationship. He allows me to sit in my laziness. He's content to wait for me, but I know He's not going to give up on a different communication style and go back to the old way just because I didn't feel like investing in the process.

And aside from knowing that sometimes I'm lazy and want someone else to do all the work for me, I can't give you a good reason why I wait, except I don't feel like it. Haven't we all said that at some point in our lives? And not even in reference to our relationship with God. We procrastinate, avoid responsibility, browse social media, or binge one episode after another of the latest Netflix series. There's a never-ending list of ways to procrastinate. But I do myself (and God) a disservice when I choose to avoid Him.

God speaks to me through dreams. While I'm asleep, He has given wisdom, provided insight, birthed new visions, and conveyed warnings. Dreams are one of my favorite ways to communicate with God. When I wake up, I remember everything. It's crystal clear. Sometimes the dream is literal, but often it is figurative. I've learned to write the dreams down as soon as I'm awake, so I don't forget them. (It's surprising how quickly I can forget—the moment I get up and my feet hit the floor, it's gone.) I spend at least one day processing with God. I ask Him for insight and think about the various elements or themes contained within the dream. I work to discern what these elements mean to me (which is generally more applicable than using a dream dictionary). It also helps to talk through the dream with someone, and usually, that's my husband. As I talk about the events contained within the dream, I receive additional clarity; something powerful happens as I say it aloud. There have been seasons of my life where I've dreamt every night. In some ways, this method of communication is easy. I receive from God. I must write down the dream and take time to process it, but He is giving me concentrated, continuous revelation.

> We must develop the ability to trust Him. The more time we spend with Him, the more we know His heart. And the more we know His heart, the more we trust Him.

The first time one of those dream seasons occurred, I thought it would stay forever. And when the dreams stopped, I was disappointed. It felt harder to find similar places of deep connection with God. I missed the conversations as I processed each dream. When I began to realize God was changing His communication style, I was discouraged, and I struggled to establish a similar life-changing connection. I wanted the dreams to return. They came back sporadically and have continued throughout the past ten years. Sometimes they occur in concentrated nightly events, but other times, they happen once every few weeks. I don't know why God changes His communication styles, but I've learned to embrace the way He speaks in the moment—communication births trust.

In similar ways, communication became the bridge to trust within our family, especially with our adopted son. Dan, Carson (our youngest son), and I traveled to South Africa in July 2015 to finalize the adoption of our son Lungelo, who was nine at the time. We met him at this orphanage one morning and spent the day learning more about him and the place he called home. Over the next six weeks, we formed the bonds of family, fulfilled the paperwork requirements, and established his US citizenship before returning home at the end of August. At first, our son was quiet. He barely whispered "yes or no" to the questions we asked. The conversation process mirrored the process of cultivating trust. Lungelo watched the way Dan and I interacted with Carson. Carson modeled a parent-child relationship. Lungelo learned he could trust us not only from our direct interaction with him but also from our interaction with Carson. As Lungelo's trust grew, he opened his heart. Sometimes this meant expressing feelings through words, but other times his expressions came through actions.

Dan and I invested in learning about our son, his home country, life at the orphanage, his backstory, and preferences. We wanted to truly know him—to develop our relationship so we could anticipate and predict his wants and needs. We longed to know him the way we understood our other children. But it was a process that involved commitment, consistency, and a willingness to embrace the process. The same is true for our relationship with God. We must develop the ability to trust Him. The more time we spend with Him, the more we know His heart. And the more we know His heart, the more we trust Him.

I can't imagine life without Lungelo. I am grateful for the way God has designed our family and for His ability to create beauty from our brokenness. God took our pain, birthed a dream, and brought us together. Our redemption story deepens my trust in Him. If God had only brought healing for our loss, it would have been more than enough. But He gave me Dan and his children. If God had stopped there, He would have exceeded my hopes and dreams. But He went further. God birthed a desire to adopt and called our son out of his brokenness. He fused us as a family. He knew. And I don't know how God works those kinds of miracles—they are almost indescribable. But if he could take me, as a widowed, single mother, and give me an incredible husband, two more children, and then bring us our adopted son, I can trust He is at work, His love runs deep, and He knows me. God knows each of His children this way. He loves you. He is at work, writing your redemption story, and He has waited for this moment to build the bonds of trust with you.

Chapter 7
Overcoming Our Trauma-Based Perspective

According to the National Council for Mental Wellbeing, 70 percent of American adults have experienced at least one traumatic event.[1] This statistic feels shocking. While we don't usually think of our difficult circumstances as traumatic events, for many of us it is the truth. The American Psychological Association states, "Trauma is an emotional response to a terrible event like an accident, rape, or natural disaster."[2] Trauma can occur during or after losing a loved one, a severe illness, or witnessing an assault. Most of us probably keep our traumatic experiences a secret. We share with relatively few people, and only after establishing deep bonds of trust. We protect ourselves and our stories out of necessity because sharing our brokenness is often painful. Not everyone can handle our stories, and there's nothing worse than sharing personal details only to realize afterward the individual we trusted can't handle our truth.

I want to be clear about the impact of trauma, and I feel it's necessary to say this up front. As we walk through the aftermath of a traumatic event, it is beneficial to talk through our experiences with a neutral individual. We derive a great benefit when we share our pain, our disappointments, and our vulnerability with someone well-trained to listen and help us navigate the road ahead. It is always a good idea to get counseling. Although I have already mentioned counseling, I felt it was essential to come back and reinforce it here. As you read through this chapter and see yourself within these pages, you may feel some of your traumatic events resurface. Please know, if this happens, it is understandable. It does not mean there's something wrong with you; it does not mean you have not found healing; it simply means you are human. However, if you feel like the reminders of your trauma or the aftermath cause a setback or are a difficult place where you cannot find the path to move forward, a counselor can help you through this process.

When we experience brokenness, it changes the way we see the world around us. It impacts our expectations, our ability to hope, and our belief that positive outcomes exist in our circumstances. I have experienced this firsthand. After losing my father, embracing the hope of a beautiful future was challenging. When his oncologist said the tumor was gone, we all knew it *could* come back. But I envisioned a different story. I could not imagine the future without my dad, so I did not allow the reality of a recurrence to exist in my mind. I am not someone who can easily admit defeat. I will hold onto hope and do everything possible to create a positive outcome. After walking through and reflecting on my life experiences, I know perspective is everything. And sometimes, what we see when we look at our circumstances is not what God sees when He looks at our lives. He's given me the courage to dig deep into healing, believe for more, and pursue every possibility. And this was precisely how I approached my dad's cancer.

When we found out his tumor was back, I still believed in his ability to overcome it. I prayed and pleaded with God for his healing. My dad began another regimen of treatments, but they took a severe toll on his already weakened body. As we approached Christmas, we all knew he could not keep up this fight much longer. He had planned to talk to his oncologist at the next appointment and arrange for palliative care. The doctors had already stated there was no cure. These treatments were merely buying time. But the price was too high. He wanted to enjoy the time he had left without the terrible side effects of his chemotherapy regimen. We knew this Christmas would be the last one we spent with him—unless he received a miracle. And while it would've been hard to lose him any day, losing him on Christmas Eve felt all-encompassing.

> When we experience brokenness, it changes the way we see the world around us. It impacts our expectations, our ability to hope, and our belief that positive outcomes exist in our circumstances.

My family loves Christmas. We always begin decorating right after Thanksgiving. On Black Friday, I swap out the regular dishes we use all year for our Christmas dishes. It's a tradition I enjoyed growing up and have continued with my family. The eight-foot Christmas tree in our living room is a showcase for the ornaments the kids have received (and made) throughout the years. Our dining room tree holds the antique ornaments that belonged to my grandparents. And you'll find a beautifully adorned tree in each bedroom. In our home, Christmas isn't a day or a week; it's a seasonal celebration where we step into the joy of relationships and the gift of friends and family. Presents are selected with extraordinary care and often without a wish list. As a mom, there's nothing better than seeing my kids' faces light up on Christmas morning as they unwrap each package. The emphasis on celebration seemed a stark contrast to the loss of my father. It was as if the two scenes (celebration and death) could not coexist in my brain.

It was hard to think about our family ever experiencing the joy of Christmas morning again. I couldn't envision embracing the Christmas season without feeling as though losing my dad on Christmas Eve forever ruined it. Every year would remind me of what we lost—it changed my view on Christmas. It's not as though this was my first experience with loss; in some ways, it was less complex than the aftermath of losing Charlie. However, it hit my heart in a way that momentarily sabotaged my hope-filled outlook and resilience.

The deep, searing pain of this loss changed me. I understood God's plan was not my plan, His timing was not my timing, and I still believed in His ability to create beauty from ashes. However, I could not, and still don't, understand why my dad died on Christmas Eve morning. And although I still loved and trusted God, I couldn't find my way through the sorrow and into the hope of a beautiful future.

The loss of my father was a traumatic event, and it brought emotional shockwaves upon me. By this point in my life, I understood the grief process and the necessity of grieving authentically. Throughout the days and weeks after, I utilized this process and allowed God to meet me in my brokenness. While I continued to heal from the pain of this loss, I struggled to maintain a positive outlook on the future. It was as if I was constantly waiting for the next bit of bad news, guarding my heart, keeping expectations low, and attempting to protect myself from further disappointment.

And while I initially thought I was protecting myself from further disappointment, the reality is I lived in it. Disappointment became a misty veil that cloaked me. As it settled over me, it was very subtle, almost unnoticeable, and I forgot it was there because of its constancy. Wherever I went, it came too. And we all do this; we say we don't want to get our hopes up, so we keep our expectations low. But there's no life there. In this place, we invite more disappointment, and it never ends. It doesn't matter what events occur, without pushing aside the veil and stepping into the hope God holds for our future, we will always perceive our circumstances through the lens of disappointment.

That's what trauma does inside of us. It changes us. It changes the way we see the world. Things that used to feel normal, conversations we used to engage in, and attitudes we used to hold, fall away. We see ourselves as outsiders in this world. And as this realization begins, we feel isolated because we think we're the only ones. We look at the people we pass in the grocery store aisle, browsing Target, and waiting for their drinks at Starbucks. They have conversations on their phone, laugh about something their friend said, and smile as they send a text. They are different from us. They seem carefree; undoubtedly, they don't know the pain we know all too well. Trauma becomes a cloak of isolation. And it only gets worse when we scroll through social media. It appears everyone else is living their best life—never experiencing anything close to the hardships that are our constant companion. Social media reinforces our perspective—we shouldn't expect anything good to happen because it's not our story. Pain and disappointment are our chapter titles, but we can't take any more bad news.

And so we stay encased in despair. And now, it doesn't just cover us; it has become our best friend. We talk to our disappointment, create a place for it to stay, and build our future on it. Disappointment tells us what we want to hear. It reinforces our pity party, pats us on the shoulder, and says we have a right to feel that way. But the story we're telling ourselves is not the truth. Everyone else knows the same pain; they just don't let us see it. If 70 percent of the American public has experienced at least one traumatic event in their lives, then almost every person we meet each day knows what we know, they feel what we feel, and they are fighting the same fight. We are not alone.

And that knowledge changes everything. We are not the only one—and we do not need to remain in the isolation of our pain.

As our perspective changes, we realize disappointment was never our friend. We call out disappointment as the liar it truly is, and we throw the cloak aside, free from the weight we've carried for so long. In this freedom, we hear God's voice and realize we haven't heard Him like this in a very long time. The covering kept His voice out. And now, He is saying, "This is not the end. Trust Me."

And that's when I truly understand I had placed my hope and trust in disappointment because I knew if I expected it, then I would not be let down. But that's not living—I was dying inside, and I stopped trusting God. This realization brought a flashback to my previous conversations on trust—all the places where God met me and taught me how to trust Him. I don't know how I forgot all those experiences. He could have scolded me, but instead, He invited me to begin again, to embrace a place of trust amid the aftermath of grief. As I walked with God in this place of faith, I realized the cloak of disappointment made my perspective darker. It was as if the sun had stopped shining. It was cloudy for so long I had forgotten how good it felt to stand in the sun.

> *If 70 percent of the American public has experienced at least one traumatic event in their lives, then almost every person we meet each day knows what we know, they feel what we feel, and they are fighting the same fight. We are not alone. And that knowledge changes everything.*

The only way we can shift from expecting more bad news to the goodness of God in our lives is to deal with our disappointment. It's not going to happen on its own, and no one else can do it for us. We are the only one who can change our perspective. But we can do it at any time; we don't have to wait for the elusive "perfect moment" because we've already told ourselves perfect moments don't apply to us. And it's like every other worthwhile but scary choice; we must do it before we believe it will work for us—we have to do it afraid.

And the truth is, choosing not to believe good things will happen doesn't protect us from future disappointment. Instead, it robs us of the ability to enjoy life right now. We can't control the future, but we can control our response to difficult people and challenging situations. We can believe God will lead us through. If we're constantly bracing ourselves for the next bad thing, we live inside the disappointment. It's not protecting us; it's destroying us.

The good news is we don't have to make the shift alone. We can invite God to meet us where we are, show us how to move forward in faith, and believe in His goodness regardless of setbacks. We lean into our friends, family members, support groups, and mental health community. We can utilize the tools we've learned to help us deal with our feelings. It's okay to be scared or unsure, but we can't stay there.

As I healed from the loss of my father and my inability to dream, I engaged in authentic conversations with a few close friends and family members. I told them I was struggling to believe in God's goodness and felt foolish because He had met me in such incredible ways after the Amish schoolhouse shooting. I knew it shouldn't be hard to believe God had good ahead, but I remained in this conflict between wishing my dad would have lived and processing all I had lost. My friends and family members didn't have answers, some were going through similar things, but they listened. And I wasn't alone in it anymore. There was something powerful that happened as I shared my struggles. It felt freeing to let my guard down and admit the reality of what I felt inside. Most of them didn't know—I had kept it hidden.

And it made me think of the others I'd judged at the grocery store, Target, and Starbucks. Many of them were probably just like me. They, too, knew trauma. They were trying to hide the reality of the weight they carried—living a life that looked normal, all the while feeling hopeless inside.

According to the National Center for PTSD, typical responses to trauma include:

- Losing hope for the future
- Feeling distant or losing concern about others
- The inability to concentrate
- Feeling on guard all the time
- Recurring dreams or memories that cause distress.

Trauma can also cause an emotional impact, such as feeling helpless, fearful, angry, agitated, and having a negative view of yourself or the world around you. In addition, you may feel physical symptoms such as trouble eating, difficulty sleeping, feeling shaky, and frequent headaches. And here's the other thing about trauma and grief: our American culture sets us up for failure. While most employers give several days off when you experience a profound loss, we assume their recovery time is just a couple of days. And nothing could be further from the truth. To effectively recover from trauma and grief, we must engage in a healing process spanning weeks, months, and even years. But no one tells us this, and we find it out the hard way when we're in the middle of a grief or trauma journey, feeling lost and alone. We think we're doing it wrong because we thought we would feel better in a matter of days or weeks, but we don't. We remember the trauma vividly when we close our eyes. We expect to get a text or phone call from the person we lost, but it never comes. We think about the conversation we'll have the next time we see them, only to realize it's not going to happen.

It's as if we must learn how to untangle them from the web that is our lives. And it's hard because the grief journey intertwines with the substance of who we are. It touches everything. The strings are hard to follow. They twist and turn in ways we didn't expect, unraveling our very selves—becoming a much more complex process than we imagined. But we must work through our grief. It's the only way we can find healing from our pain; we can't push it aside and pretend it doesn't exist. We can't tell ourselves it's been a few weeks, and we need to move on. We must embrace the process. And knowing it takes weeks, months, and years gives us permission to take our time. Grief cannot be rushed, and healing does not occur on our timetable, and that's okay because we can only handle one small piece at a time.

First, it seems like nothing is happening. Even if we have one good day, it feels overshadowed by several difficult ones afterward. But as the weeks progress, and we look back, we can see there are more good days than bad ones. That's what it looked like for me as I dealt with the death of my first daughter. Her death was my first personal experience with grief. I had nothing else to base this journey on, which was frustrating. Some people told me it had been a month and I should move on; others asked why I still felt periods of sadness after just six weeks. I thought they were right, and I was doing this whole grief thing incorrectly. But since then, I've realized I didn't process my grief wrong; their expectations didn't match reality.

If you've had the same experience with people challenging your time frame, asking why you're still sad or hinting you should be able to move on by now, it's probably time to close the door to that relationship. Or at least refuse to allow their comments to impact the way you think about yourself. We need an actual support system as we process our loss and deal with our grief. We need to trust we can lean into our friends and family when needed. And while most of the time, we can heal from the trauma on our own, it's also essential to include the help of trained professionals as needed. As much as we all like the illusion of control, grief and trauma are things we cannot control; it's as if we surrender to the process and yield ourselves to the pain, joy, and journey.

Sometimes I think about how my journey would have looked different had I understood what happens inside us when we experience trauma before I found myself in its grasp. It's not that knowing these things makes it easier, but it would have made it less complicated. I still would have had to journey through the heartache and find myself on the other side, but I wouldn't have expected it to occur quickly. I would have been okay knowing it was a process. And so, I hope hearing me say those words helps you. It is a process, and you will get through it. The most important thing is to take each day as one step on your journey. You only have to take one step at a time.

Successfully navigating the process requires a willingness to invest in self-care. And while it may be challenging to engage in the things that usually bring you joy, force yourself to do it. Plan to meet a friend for coffee, invite yourself to your parents' house for dinner, take a walk and listen to the birds. Use the self-care strategies discussed in previous chapters to help you through this section of your life. Listen to a guided imagery meditation narration online, find an art and mindfulness exercise tutorial, or bake a favorite recipe. Write down your thoughts. Your journal is a safe place where you can ask your unanswerable questions and write them as a letter to God or to the person you lost. Writing is healing. No one cares about your grammar, and perfection is not the point. Just let your feelings out. And as you do these things, invite God into the process.

Let Him meet you in the coffee shop, or as you drive to your parents' house. Ask Him to join you while walking, painting, or baking. Invite Him to speak His words of life and hope and love over you. Soak in them. Write them down so you can come back to them later. And one day, when you least expect it, you'll start to dream again. You'll find hope within your heart that speaks to the shift occurring as you think about the future. It will probably catch you by surprise, and you'll look back thinking you had no idea it was there, but it is.

If you find yourself in the pages of this chapter and identify with an inability to believe God has good things planned for your future, embrace the part of the journey right where you are. I know grief is not convenient. And you probably don't feel like doing the work it's going to take to get the healing you need. You are strong enough to navigate this journey, and it will probably take less time than you think. Embrace it, if for no other reason than because you deserve what's coming on the other side. You deserve more than what you know right now.

Chapter 8
Choosing Forgiveness

If there's one thing that has impacted me more than almost anything else, it's forgiveness. But before I explain how forgiveness has altered the trajectory of my life, I want to share a few foundational thoughts. Choosing forgiveness does not mean there are no consequences for an action that hurts us. Forgiveness does not exclude a perpetrator from punishment, eliminate necessary boundaries, or require us to embrace a place where we will be wounded again. Forgiveness doesn't focus on the one who wounded us. Forgiveness occurs between my heart and God. It's an experience (or series of experiences) which enable healing, but it has nothing to do with the other person.

However, this wasn't always my perspective. As a little girl growing up in a conservative, rural area of the country, what I learned or how I interpreted forgiveness was different. I thought forgiveness happened when someone who had hurt me recognized the wound they had caused. They authentically wanted to help me find healing and restore our relationship. So they would come, apologize, and do whatever was necessary to regain my trust. But often, the person who has wounded us doesn't come.

Either they aren't aware of the hurt they have caused, or they don't care. In the aftermath of the Amish schoolhouse shooting, my choice to forgive Charlie, and the Amish communities' choice to forgive Charlie, was not about Charlie.

A few hours after the shooting, I was at my parents' house, looking out their kitchen window. I was thinking about the way my life had so dramatically changed. I couldn't understand how I woke up that morning, a stay-at-home mom with three kids, and by lunchtime, I was a widowed single mother. And it's not just that I was a single mom. It was the way he chose to leave. As I thought about these things, I saw some Amish men walking down the street. I knew they were coming to my parents' home; this was the town I had grown up in, and we were not strangers. I told my parents about the Amish men and said I didn't know what to do. I had nothing to give them, no answers to any questions. My dad said I should stay inside and offered to go outside and talk with them. I could not hear what they were saying, but I saw everything through the window. I saw the way they put their hands on my dad's shoulders, the tears that flowed down everyone's faces, and the way they embraced him before they walked away. When he came inside, we waited for him to collect himself from the emotion of their conversation. He said, "Marie, they came because they were concerned about you and your children, and they wanted you to know they had forgiven Charlie. They are extending grace and compassion over your family."

I was stunned! They did not come to get anything from me. They made no demands and asked no questions; instead, they came to give a gift—forgiveness and its impact. I knew I, too, had

> *Forgiveness doesn't focus on the one who wounded us. Forgiveness occurs between my heart and God. It's an experience (or series of experiences) which enable healing, but it has nothing to do with the other person.*

to forgive Charlie. I would inevitably pour the contents of my heart upon my children. Even more now than before, I wanted to love my kids authentically, saturate them with hope, and help them heal despite our devastation. I could not accomplish those goals if my heart were full of unforgiveness and anger toward Charlie, but he was not part of the forgiveness process. And this one experience changed everything I thought I knew about forgiveness. It wasn't an instantaneous event. Instead, it involved me coming to God with my brokenness over and over. Each time, He took the process a little deeper.

Often, I didn't know the pain and the healing were coming. They came unexpectedly, like grief, but looking back, I see a pattern. As I worked through challenges with my kids or when their loss was highly noticeable, I felt their anguish. I tried to stay in tune with their well-being. I was aware of the trauma we were all working to overcome, but seeing my kids in pain broke me in a way that was different from my emotions. There were many times when I wished I could stand in front of Charlie and demand answers, "Why did you do this to our children, to me, to the Amish families, our families, and our community?" But I couldn't talk about it with Charlie. Instead, I spoke to God. "God, I don't understand why he did this. I'm frustrated that he would purposefully inflict this level of pain on so many people. Why would he do this to our children? How will they heal and move on from this moment?" As I met God in the vulnerability of brokenness, He helped me forgive Charlie, piece by piece. And forgiveness is another place where we must relinquish control. There isn't a recipe for a list of predictable steps which guarantee the desired outcome. Much like the grieving process, forgiveness is complicated, and we do not control it. While we may be able to identify specific circumstances or conditions that remind us of our pain in a more significant way—ultimately leading to a place of more profound forgiveness—moments like these are often unpredictable. And they don't come when we feel like making room for them. They demand our full attention whether we like it or not.

And it's okay to tell God you don't feel like embracing this process. He understands. He sees our hearts and knows the intensity of the world around us. He will enable us to make the space necessary for our healing, but He is far more concerned with the process than the next task on our list. There have been many days where I've met Him in this place, not because it was my idea, but because I've learned to trust His invitation. It's in those moments where emotion exists just below the surface. It was an overwhelming feeling I could not escape. I could either choose to embrace it or try to push it away.

If I pushed it away, it would come back later, but if I chose to embrace it, I would find healing. And while we might only choose to embrace it and meet with God out of obligation, He doesn't hold our attitude against us. And He doesn't bring us back to traumatic memories to cause pain. God is a good father who loves His children and loves us enough to allow us to experience momentary discomfort because it's the bridge between the pain of our past and hope in the future.

He knows it is worth the inconvenience to our schedule and the reminder of our brokenness. We see ourselves, others, and God differently when looking at life through the lens of healing. We identify the way God met us in our broken place. He gives us perspective as we look back on what we couldn't see while walking through it. It changes our belief about the experience, who we are because of it, and the way God walked us through it.

Choosing to forgive Charlie didn't mean he wasn't responsible for his actions, but it allowed me to live outside of the sorrow I felt about choices. Charlie was still responsible, and if he had not taken his own life, responsibility and punishment would have played out through the judicial system. Since he committed suicide, my situation is different than someone who has experienced abuse and knows they will face their abuser in the future. I want to pause on this for a moment because I'm often asked questions regarding forgiveness and situations of abuse. In some cultures, authority figures strongly encourage (or force) victims to express forgiveness toward their abuser and maintain a relationship with the accused, but this is wrong. It infers the victim has no value, and their pain is acceptable. It further suggests the victim is the guilty party (often called "the sin of unforgiveness") if they refuse to participate in a relationship with the abuser. Instead of holding the abuser accountable for their actions, those in authority force the victim into a relationship through the guise of restoration. Those who demand they forgive are not actively investing in the victim's security.

Acts like these are not God's heart. God does not mandate a type of forgiveness that places us in danger of physical, mental, or emotional harm. Instead, He offers the opportunity to exchange our brokenness for His healing. But this process of forgiveness is bathed in God's love and compassion for us. He loves us enough to ask us to step into our pain so He can pour out His healing. It's not easy for Him to see us in pain, but He knows that while the pain is temporary, the healing will become transformational.

A few years ago, my son, Bryce, broke and dislocated a small, delicate bone in his wrist (the lunate). He underwent emergency surgery to repair the break. Several pins held the bones in place as his wrist healed. After completing the healing process, he began physical therapy to regain the movement and strength lost during immobilization. I knew therapy was painful, and at first, it didn't seem to make any noticeable difference. He wanted to quit, but I encouraged him to continue. I didn't allow him to give up on his healing. He was too young to endure life defined by limitation. After several grueling weeks filled with therapy appointments, frustration, and doubt, he noticed improvement.

It was stunning, and it made the pain caused by the exercises worthwhile.

And similarly, God knows the healing we find through forgiveness will help us see our pain differently. I'm grateful for the way forgiveness intersected my life. Now, I look back at my definition of forgiveness, pre-2006, and realize I had it all wrong. Forgiveness is not about the other person. At its core, forgiveness is about me.

A restored relationship may be a peripheral outcome of the process, but it is not the focus. Forgiveness doesn't take away the need for boundaries. Extending forgiveness does not mean you don't have a right to protect yourself. It simply means you want to live outside the weight of pain, anger, and shame. Forgiveness brings freedom. Had I not chosen to forgive Charlie, I wouldn't have been able to cultivate a healthy relationship with my husband, Dan. If I had filled my perspective with unforgiveness, I would have sabotaged our relationship with skepticism and doubt. I would have expected Dan to make similar choices. A lack of trust would have undermined any hope of a redemptive future for our family.

There are two other types of forgiveness I want to discuss. We must learn to forgive ourselves, and at some point in life we will need to ask for forgiveness from others. In both instances, we are the ones who have done something "wrong." I say this loosely because the struggle with forgiving ourselves often comes from a misguided perspective on what we've done wrong. We're our harshest critics. We set unreasonable expectations and tell ourselves we are a failure when we don't achieve the impossible. We set ourselves up for future self-sabotage. But instead, it should lead us to self-forgiveness. And while our first thought may be that we need to forgive our failure to achieve the desired outcome; the place where we actually need to extend forgiveness to ourselves is in the initial expectation. We must forgive ourselves for creating a scenario where failure was the only option.

The outcome of forgiveness is not merely the act but the change that occurs afterward. When I forgive someone, there is change—the one who hurt me must rebuild my trust, and I will approach the relationship differently until it occurs. I may decide there are other boundaries necessary for my protection or there must be evidence of a change within them, not just their words stating it won't happen again. Similarly, there must also be evidence of change when I forgive myself. I must change how I determine appropriate expectations; I will give myself additional time to complete tasks, create checkpoints along the way, and revise time frames as needed. I give myself

Forgiveness doesn't take away the need for boundaries. Extending forgiveness does not mean you don't have a right to protect yourself. It simply means you want to live outside the weight of pain, anger, and shame. Forgiveness brings freedom.

grace. Forgiveness brings change, and I can't give myself a free pass on personal transformation. If we forgive someone over and over for the same hurtful actions, it won't be long before we decide to distance ourselves from our relationship with them because we know their statements regarding change were not sincere. But we allow this with ourselves all the time. We don't institute a strategy for necessary change.

We don't hold ourselves accountable because it's as if we don't have any respect for ourselves. When we require another person to make healthy, appropriate changes to remain in relationship with us, we act out of self-respect. However, when we need to change the way we think about ourselves, the expectations (and demands) we place on ourselves, and the negative self-talk we allow, we often don't hold ourselves accountable. This perspective comes through forgiveness and the realization we wouldn't let others treat us the way we treat ourselves.

My inner voice is unkind and demanding, and I won't ever finish my self-imposed to-do list. It's no wonder I assume others think the worst of me—I do it to myself all the time. And for most of my adult life (thus far), I let these behaviors continue without question. But through a season of personal reflection, I started to see it differently. Based on what I've read in the Bible and experienced, I know God loves me. However, I couldn't engage in life from a place of God's constant love. I lived in a place of self-sabotage and negative self-talk.

And then, I realized if I want to authentically believe God loves me, my husband loves me, and any other person truly loves me, I need to love myself. We won't believe we are worth being loved by another person (or God) if we are incapable of loving ourselves. Self-love is not a mystical process. It's not a new-age mantra, and it's not optional. If we've reinforced self-disappointment, self-criticism, and condemnation, we've significantly reduced (or eliminated) our ability to feel love. Each time God or another person attempts to love us, we will dismiss it. We tell ourselves things like, "They don't mean it. They are just saying it because they feel obligated. They only say they love me when they want something."

Self-love starts with forgiveness. As we forgive ourselves for places of past disappointments, things we should have done differently, and times when we hurt someone, we free ourselves from self-hatred and open the doors to self-love. But there's still more to do. The repetitive nature of our unkind, demanding, and demeaning thoughts has formed deep ruts in our brain. If we don't work to create a new pathway, we'll get sucked back into the well-worn track.

I can't imagine how God feels when He hears the way we talk about ourselves. As a parent, if one of my kids said things such as, "I'm such a failure, I'm never going to be the kind of person I want to be, and I'm just going to keep messing up for the rest of my life," I would be ready to launch an intervention. I wouldn't use subjective terms like telling them they were terrific or intelligent. Instead, I would give them specific reasons why they were more than their demeaning statements. I would start with their positive attributes and give specific examples. "You are an amazing friend—you see the pain in another's life, and you do something about it. You're a great coach—I couldn't have navigated that ski slope without you. You are thoughtful—your brother loved the shoes you picked for him." And we must do the same for ourselves.

It feels silly when you work through it the first few times, but it is effective. As I've used this process with myself, I have replaced the demanding, critical voice in my head with one that is much gentler, and I've also increased my self-confidence. Identifying my strengths is easier and I don't feel guilty about my weaknesses. This process has changed everything for me. Positive self-talk follows forgiveness. Before I experienced this transformation, I was constantly looking for someone to affirm me, because I was insecure. However, even when I received the affirmation I longed for, it didn't make a lasting impact because I dismissed it.

But now, I can speak positive words over myself, and I believe them. Here's what this sounds like, "I'm a visionary—I see opportunity when others see a struggle. I'm a great problem solver—I can take the outcome and create a plan by working backwards. I'm a good listener and know how to ask the right question. I have a high level of motivation—I'll identify a huge goal and go after it tenaciously. I don't give up—just because it's hard doesn't mean I can't do it." And just like all the other exercises we've done together, it can help to approach this one objectively. "If this wasn't my life, if it belonged to a friend, what would I say were her strengths?" And if you're stuck, ask a friend for her insight!

As you work through this process, invite God into the conversation. Ask Him to help you identify your strengths. Ask for His insight, do this in one of the places you've explored through earlier chapters in this book, such as guided imagery, meditation, mindfulness, or while walking outside. Remember, if you struggle to sit still while praying, find another method that works for you!

This brings us to the last aspect of forgiveness—asking another person to forgive us. I'll be the first to admit this is hard. It's difficult to accept we have caused pain, especially when it was not intentional. I remember a season of parenting when it felt like one of my kids constantly complained the other one had hurt them. And it wasn't defined to a particular child. They were all guilty of inflicting harm. But often, the way the impacted sibling received it wasn't the way the initiator intended. I remember hearing the standard line, "I didn't mean it," almost daily. And I always replied the same way, "Just because you didn't mean to hurt them doesn't mean your words and actions didn't cause pain." Then we talked about what they needed to do to fix it. Sometimes restoration happened just by saying they were sorry. But often, the injured sibling didn't want to associate with the offender for at least a few hours.

This situation occurred because they needed space to process, time to forgive, or the ability to see the remorse expressed was authentic. And while grown-up problems or situations that require adult forgiveness are more complicated than those of five- and eight-year-old siblings, the premise is the same. We must embrace a place of humility where our remorse is authentic—the "I'm sorry" must be sincere. We can begin by asking God to help us see this situation from the other person's perspective. As we embrace their point of view, we can think back over our conversation or actions (whatever caused harm) and objectively determine where we were at fault and how we should proceed. While the entire outcome may not be our fault, we own our responsibility for it. We apologize and allow them to interject into the conversation. The ultimate goal is a greater understanding of one another and deeper trust. However, it doesn't always work out this way. Although we own our responsibility, forgiveness and restoration do not include coercion or manipulation. The other individual should not make us feel condemned, guilty of more than our responsibility, or shame. If the conversation falls apart in the process of seeking forgiveness, or you start to feel the weight of their words as shame, guilt, or condemnation, your role moves from restoration to protection of your heart and mind. Their response is ultimately their responsibility. You may seek forgiveness in the best possible way and not end up with the desired outcome. They may not be ready to extend forgiveness and need time to process your words and respond later. They could be dealing with other issues that make it difficult for them to respond to you. But all these things, and the specifics for their response, do not fall upon your shoulders. You own your actions, and they must own theirs.

Forgiveness is complicated, and it's not a one-time event. It is often a process that continues and resurfaces when we least expect it. But forgiveness is a gift. It changes us, the way we see ourselves, and the way we see others—and that changes everything.

Chapter 9
Developing an Action Plan

If you've made it this far, you've worked through an extensive list of intense concepts. You've created mindset strategies, addressed negative self-talk, and reframed self-sabotage. You've embraced the courage to dream again, celebrated all the small steps, welcomed God into your process, adjusted trauma-based perspectives, and focused on forgiveness. If we look at the strategies in this book as a home renovation, you've essentially stripped the walls down to the bare studs, removed all the carpet, and upgraded the electrical and plumbing. You've taken the house down to the foundation, addressed the structure, and are ready to begin rebuilding. This section is where it gets good. It's finally the fun part! You get to pick new cabinets, flooring, and light fixtures. You can create your dream kitchen or luxurious master bath. But you couldn't experience all the fun of this stage if you didn't do all the hard work first. Take a deep breath, grab your journal and a favorite beverage, and let's get started on the second half.

Here is where we develop our action plan. It's the framework of all that is to come, and in this section, we will utilize the tools gained in previous chapters. What do you want most from this season of life? When you read through the chapter on dreams, was there one dream that resurfaced? It may be time to accomplish a goal you've thought about over the last decade. Maybe you've felt the spark of a new dream or a new season—you're starting fresh with a blank page. If you're wondering whether you're doing this right, remove those thoughts from your brain, and tell yourself, "This is where I'm supposed to be—this is right; this is my starting line." It's your race. You are the only competitor and don't have to set a record. Instead, you can choose to enjoy the journey. Let's begin.

We're going to start by gathering a new dream. If you feel uncertain of your next step, engage in your favorite creative outlet. Take a walk while you listen to music, bake your favorite cookies, paint, draw, dance, or play an instrument. Engaging in a creative process helps to remove the feeling of being "stuck." As you create, ask God to speak. Tell Him you need His help understanding this next part of your journey. You're choosing to lay aside everything you tell yourself you "should" do to find the thing that will ignite passion and wonder inside of you. And then create without any pressure to discover this "thing." Let it find you.

My creative place is the first activity I mentioned—taking a walk while I listen to music. Earlier this year, our family brought home a puppy, a Newfoundland/Malamute mix named Bruno. As I write this, he's almost one year old, weighs 115 lbs., and is about my height when he stands on his hind legs. Bruno needs a lot of exercise. Don't let the Newfoundland part of his breeding fool you. He's all Malamute when it comes to activity level. I've gotten into the habit of taking him on four walks each day. And while I initially thought I was doing this for Bruno, I quickly realized God was doing this for me.

I've found life-altering inspiration on those walks. I pop one AirPod in, hit my favorite Amazon Music station (Elevation

Worship), and off we go. (Side note: I use one AirPod so I can still hear my neighbors if they initiate a conversation.) On these walks, I talk to God, embrace the refreshing qualities of worship music, and get out of the limitations within my head. The inspiration for this book came through a walk on September 25, 2022. I was tired, and I told God how I felt. I recently completed a four-year bachelor's degree in Organizational Behavior in two and a half years while maintaining a 4.0 GPA, building my coaching/consulting business, and staying invested as a mom and wife. Now I am working to grow the organizational consulting side of my work (Elevated Solutions Consulting). It's not that I didn't know it would require hard work, an intense level of commitment, and consistent implementation of new ideas, but I didn't realize how grueling it would feel. I told God I was tired of "hard," and I just wanted a season of "easy."

But I know "easy" doesn't exist. I knew I was asking for the impossible; because honestly, I wouldn't like easy. I love challenges. They fuel me. There's nothing like the thought of conquering something almost impossible to get my brain going and inspire creativity within me. Looking back at our conversation, more than anything, I probably needed a nap. And I'm grateful God knows me well enough to realize I didn't even want what I asked. Instead, as I finished explaining why I was so tired, I felt His response—write a book. He had my attention.

While I was engaged in various small projects since the completion of my degree, I didn't have a big one, and this contributed to my exhaustion. Big projects, or what I refer to as my keystone goal, drive me. It's the one thing that holds everything else in place. For me, the keystone provides stability. This project became my keystone. And while nothing changed about the day-to-day (except I was still doing everything else and now squeezing in a few hours of daily writing), everything changed. I felt a sense of confidence and purpose I had missed. I saw the way God wove pieces of my life experience, faith perspective, and psychology into the same tapestry, and it fueled me.

My standard goal-setting practice involves identifying the keystone goal and structuring everything around it. While pursuing my degree, education was my keystone goal. But once I graduated college, I forgot I needed to designate a new keystone. I attribute it to a rigorously paced course schedule and a keystone goal that remained constant over thirty months. When my classes ended, I told myself I needed a break. And then, I moved on to establish my business and connect with new clients without recognizing I had forgotten about the keystone.

If you haven't thought of goals this way, it's not as complicated as it might seem. Write a list of your responsibilities, dreams, and goals on a page in your journal. Then look for similarities. Jot some notes based on the similarities or themes you identify. As you think about the themes, pick one that brings everything together. For example, while I was in school, the main themes were schoolwork, coaching/consulting, speaking events, family, and household responsibilities. I knew schoolwork was the key because I had to work my speaking/consulting schedules around it. Also, I emphasized accomplishing as much schoolwork as possible outside of designated family time. School took priority.

But sometimes, the keystone goal makes all the other goals possible. Our goals should include a focus on the following:

- mental well-being (through counseling)
- creating healthy eating habits
- instituting boundaries that protect us from unhealthy relationships
- rebuilding our trust in God

Our focus on mental well-being (counseling) would be the keystone goal. The other goals are secondary. As we focus on well-being, we'll be better able to make healthy choices in all areas, including eating habits, boundaries, and trust in God. Creating an action plan begins with identifying the keystone goal but doesn't end there.

We must then break the larger goal down into daily action steps. An overall, significant goal can feel elusive or impossible. When we take the big goal and break it into small pieces, it becomes possible. We must believe the goal is achievable. Otherwise, no amount of motivation or willpower will ensure success. If my goal is mental well-being, then in addition to counseling appointments I'll need to utilize other techniques such as reading inspirational books, engaging in mindset-enhancing activities and journaling (my secondary goals). Then I'll break those down into daily action steps. I'd listen to an audiobook for thirty minutes each day while getting ready for work each morning, journal my thoughts at the end of the workday (ten minutes), and spend ten to fifteen minutes before bed on meditation/guided imagery.

Once we identify our keystone goal, secondary goals, and small steps, we can use them to determine identifiable outcomes that help us track our progress. We can create a tracking system more easily when it corresponds to a number (such as losing a specific number of pounds, drinking a certain amount of water, or time spent in self-care). It's more challenging to track abstract concepts such as mental well-being, boundaries, or trust, but it's possible. We determine markers along to way to strengthen mental well-being by working with our counselor. We can determine progress in our relationship with God through moments of reflection. One way to create mini-goals and track outcomes for strengthened mental well-being could be as simple as committing to regular counseling appointments for at least six months.

Before I used the keystone goal strategy, I've tried to change everything simultaneously, but I discovered this is overwhelming. While I may think it would be possible to schedule counseling appointments, commit to a radical eating overhaul, and institute boundaries with all out-of-control relationships at once, it's not a plan that leads me to success. Instead, those times become experiences where my unreasonable expectations set me up for failure. It's best to take on an additional goal once I feel comfortable with the first goal. In this scenario, I would schedule several counseling appointments and work through at least the first two before I added additional mini goals. Then I would work to prioritize goals relating to diet—increasing water and decreasing coffee. After successfully rehabbing my daily beverage consumption, I would work to reduce processed foods and increase vegetables. I would continue adding a new goal from my list only after successfully incorporating a previous goal for at least ten days. For me, a week isn't long enough to feel confident I won't revert to past behavior. I must make it through a weekend and into the following week before I am certain I can continue long-term.

> *An overall, significant goal can feel elusive or impossible. When we take the big goal and break it into small pieces, it becomes possible.*

Take some time to think about the way goals have (and have not) worked for you in the past. Even if most of your goal experiences have felt disappointing, it does not mean you are a failure or can't achieve your goals. Remember, we can view past attempts as learning opportunities instead of successes or failures. This shift has been a huge growth point for me. I grew up with a perfectionist mindset. If I didn't do something perfectly, I felt like I was a failure. I was constantly replaying a very negative (and sabotaging) line of self-talk.

In the past few years, I've challenged myself to look for growth instead of perfection. Mastery doesn't occur the first time. What matters is we keep trying. This is our life. We are the only ones who can change it. As we begin the steps necessary to achieve our goals, our previous lessons on mindset, negative self-talk, self-sabotage, and celebration are key. Too often, we relegate the celebration to the ending instead of incorporating it throughout the entire process. As we look for our small wins and celebrate them, we begin to pave a new pathway in our brain. Instead of falling into the rut of negative self-talk, we embark on a new road that identifies our successes. In the keystone goal of mental well-being, we would celebrate our counseling sessions and follow-up work. In our process to replace coffee with water, we would celebrate a week of achieving our daily water goal. And yes, it's essential to incorporate rewards.

It's the same as we begin working toward our goals. Often, we need a reward for a low level of effort. It reinforces our capability. But then, after we've achieved the low level, we move the reward. Now we must do a bit more to get what we want. The reward type depends on your preference, but it must feel meaningful to you. Maybe you'd love to spend several hours on a Saturday afternoon curled up in your favorite chair, a cup of jasmine tea on the table beside you, with the book you've wanted to read for months, finally in your hands. That's a great reward! Or maybe, you'd love to catch up with your best friend at your local coffee shop while you sip a seasonal latte—also a great reward. Or maybe you love to create the perfect cocktail for you and your husband—fabulous! The point is this: whatever feels motivating to you is the right choice. Most of us are motivated by achieving something that brings pleasure.

However, some of us are motivated by avoiding pain. If you fall into this category, your reward takes some additional thought. If you don't reduce your coffee addiction and replace your caffeinated beverage with water, you'll feel shaky, your heartbeat may flutter irregularly, and you'll feel tired in the afternoon. You especially hate it when your heartbeat gets out of rhythm, even if it is only for a few moments. You know you feel more energetic and focused in the afternoon when you've had at least twenty ounces of water by noon. So, you remind yourself drinking water helps you to avoid heartbeat issues and helps you have the energy you need to remain focused through the afternoon.

You get to determine your reward. Do you have a new pair of shoes in the shopping cart on your favorite website—there's your motivation! Have you wanted to spend a leisurely afternoon at the contemporary art exhibit? That's perfect. Have fun with your reward. Embrace simplicity or extravagance. Start with a reward that ensures motivation and consistency—for no longer than one week. Then scale back the reward or extend the time (not both simultaneously). I enjoy shopping and finding a great deal, which ties into my love language of gifts. I can incorporate these dimensions by shopping Amazon Warehouse deals (my favorite) for a new pair of shoes. Part of the thrill for me is how much money I save. I know the fun of the adventure is part of the reward. When using this method, I'll set my time frame for the goal (a week to ten days), and then when I fulfill the parameters, I give myself thirty minutes to an hour to shop for shoes that cost $15 or less. It works for me, but I had to take the time to think through my reward preferences to find something that authentically felt "fun" and piqued my interest in the goal when I wasn't otherwise motivated.

I've worked through a variety of reward styles before determining what is most effective. When I've chosen something that doesn't feel meaningful, it becomes an opportunity to better understand my preferences. And the same is true for you. It will probably take several attempts to determine what has the most significant impact. Write your thoughts in your journal/notebook as you work toward identifying your reward. This process gives the ability to look back and review the effect. You might find a reward which combines several elements of previous attempts is what works best for you.

However, we must avoid the comparison trap while identifying our goals, working toward them, and instituting rewards. We are unique. There isn't another person with the same personality traits, cultural impact, environmental influences, and motivational factors we each embody. My goal or reward preferences might sound overwhelming to you. It doesn't mean either of us is wrong. We have the freedom to do what works best for us. We can give ourselves grace for the learning process. We can take the methods and practices suggested by those around us and tailor them to fit us.

While we can create and control this process, we are not alone in it. Jesus is our keystone. God's the one who makes everything else work—He holds us together. He speaks wisdom and strength when our circumstances deplete us. He sparks the hope of a new dream when we lose passion and purpose. He walks it out with us. And we don't have to force it. He offers the opportunity to rest, surrender, and hand over our dreams. He takes our stress in every moment. He will carry it. And He takes the small steps of our effort and multiplies it.

When we look at our lives, and we see the difficulties. We see our brokenness and the scars left behind. If you feel like I did on September 25, too tired to do one more thing, rest in Him. Allow Him to breathe fresh hope and faith deep within your heart. Let Him change your perspective. Yes, He's allowed you to walk through the hard parts, but it's not the end. And yes, you're different now, but different isn't always bad. Sometimes different is good. I'm a different person than I was before the Amish schoolhouse shooting. But now, I'm tenacious in a way I didn't have the courage for pre-October 2006. If God could take the broken pieces of my life and use them so I can dream new dreams and conquer fulfilling goals, He can do the same for you.

It comes down to a few simple steps. Resist the pressure to figure it out on your own and feel like you have to see the whole process before taking one step. Rest, nourish your creativity, and allow God to speak one small dream which lights a spark in your heart. Then fight the urge to line up all the steps—take the first one. Lean into Him and let Him walk with you. Let Him carry the weight of the outcome. Find the fun, create joy, and celebrate every step. You matter.

Chapter 10
Persevering through the Middle

When I think about the most enjoyable parts of any project, the beginning and the end come to mind. We feel exuberant at the start of something new due to positive emotion and excitement for the road ahead. As we come down the home stretch, we are eager to finish and feel a sense of pride in our accomplishments. But sandwiched between the excitement of the beginning and the anticipation of the end, is the middle. The middle is where any project gets tough. It's where we doubt ourselves and often the place we are most likely to give up. Have you ever decided to clean your closet or, better yet, the basement? Those are some of my most frustrating middle experiences. Last fall, I decided to clean out half of the walk-in closet my husband and I share. Well, it wasn't a decision made by desire as much as I didn't have a choice. My closet shelf detached from the wall. It was a Friday afternoon in early November, and I was in the kitchen prepping dinner. I heard a horrendous noise and ran to the closet. I arrived just in time to watch the boxes slide down the shelf that now looked like a slide. It was attached only at one end, as all the middle supports and the other side had pulled out of the wall. I knew what was coming. There was no denying it, and this was not how I wanted to spend my weekend.

I'll be honest—I had entirely too many things (I never wore) hanging from the rack. I also had a sizable collection of boxes stacked on the attached shelf. It was no surprise the wall anchors couldn't support the weight. I tried to convince myself this would be an enjoyable project with various benefits. It would force me to part with clothing I wouldn't wear again, allowing me to finally organize my wardrobe. I began by taking everything out of the closet—each pair of shoes, all the bags, and clothing. Then there were the hanging storage organizers. I piled my things in wash baskets so I wouldn't have to make so many trips from the closet into my bedroom. By the time I finished emptying my side of the closet, I wanted to close the closet door and pretend it never happened, but I was pretty sure my husband wouldn't think it was a good idea. When he got home from work, I showed him the disaster area, and he began planning a trip to our local hardware store.

Dan spent Saturday morning attaching new wall anchors to the studs, securing the supports for the shelf unit, and double-checking that everything was level. Then it was time for me to put my clothing away. I like to keep everything (just in case) but decided to give it my best "Marie Kondo" attempt so I wouldn't risk destroying the closet again. I made three piles—keep, donate, and I'm not sure. At first, sorting clothes, shoes, and accessories went well because I began with easy items. It wasn't hard to sort when I knew the pieces were going in the keep or donate piles. The accumulation of the "I'm not sure" category was my downfall. Just when I thought I had finished, I realized there were several baskets of random items I had shoved in the back of my closet. For a moment, I thought about either stuffing it all back in (the way it was) or throwing everything away. I didn't want to take the time necessary to sort through it. I was stuck in the middle of the project while wishing I was at the end. And there wasn't a shortcut. The only way to get to the end goal (a decently organized closet) was by working through it step-by-step. This experience reminded me why my kids hate it when I say, "Let's clean the basement." They know we never really finish it. We've been "cleaning the basement" for about fifteen years, stuck in the middle of a process that, without a dumpster, has no easy ending.

And goals can feel the same way. It doesn't matter what kind of project you've embarked on; the middle feels endless. You're so far away from the excitement of the ending, and you can't seem to reach back to grab the emotional high you felt at the beginning. The middle is where we give up. It is where we question ourselves, allow doubt to seep in, and tell ourselves this was a mistake. It happens as we pursue any (and often every) goal. I've felt that way in business, while pursuing ministry opportunities, working on home projects, throughout parenting, and during childbirth. I remember joking with my midwife during the "transition phase" of labor. I asked if it was too late to change my mind because I was sure the process of delivering this baby was not a good idea.

I couldn't quit in the middle of labor, but I have abandoned other projects in the middle stage. In my current season of life, I know how the middle works. Wanting to quit is a normal part of the process. But I also know just because I want to stop doesn't mean I should. And more than that, I don't need to quit because I can accomplish the task. Looking back, I wish I had understood this decades ago. The middle is long. Much longer than we thought, you hardly enjoy the emotional high of the beginning before you're stuck in the middle—it sucks you in, and there's no escaping.

The middle part, like the transition phase of labor, is where ALL the big things happen, but we can't see it. Instead, we assume nothing is happening. We feel lost and alone and frustrated that we're lost and alone. Because we thought we'd be at the end by now, stretched out on a lounge chair, enjoying the view, with our feet propped up and our favorite beverage in our hands. We envisioned celebrating our success with the people who matter most; instead, we're stuck, isolated in the middle of something we don't want anymore.

But no one tells us this will happen, and maybe it's because they thought they were the only ones who experienced the agony of the middle. Or perhaps it's because they didn't want to ruin our enthusiasm. They saw the starry-eyed wonder radiating from our faces and thought, *I don't want to destroy that feeling. It won't last long, so I'll let her enjoy it.* But I'm giving it to you straight. I don't know about you, but I'd rather have a small dose of reality on the back side of wonder. A sweet, little moment where my friend tells me the truth. The middle is like quicksand or the phone call with your great-aunt who won't let you hang up. You're going to feel trapped but stick it out because you can get through it. And there's something incredible shifting inside of you during the middle. It's not a glamorous place. And you will probably feel like you're alone. But remind yourself you knew it was coming, and you must keep going.

> The middle is closer to the end than we were in the beginning. We are making progress.

The middle is also where we tell ourselves we must not have heard God. We criticize our ability to hear His voice, damaging our relationship with Him. It's the place where we start to add an inflection of cynicism. It's as if we are punishing God for abandoning us in the middle of this wasteland. But He hasn't left us. The problem is we have lost our sense of purpose and feel confused about the process. It's not as if someone tosses us a guidebook when we embark on a new dream or goal. There isn't a ten-step system to ensure systematic and predictable progress, and no one is celebrating that we haven't quit. Our society celebrates beginnings and endings. We don't celebrate the tenacity it takes to stick it out when we're in an endless middle section. And since we don't celebrate it, we assume God's not celebrating us either. We think He's silent, which only reinforces our isolation. But it's the opposite. God is cheering for us. He is encouraging us to continue taking one step at a time. He is whispering new strategies, fresh doses of wisdom and clarity. But when we've entered a place of self-pity, telling ourselves we are alone and no one cares, we've effectively eliminated His voice.

However, the opportunity for transformation is within our reach. Here's the secret: we can decide the middle is worthwhile and we will finish. Whatever we decide will become our truth. When I tell myself I'm stuck. It becomes my reality. But when I tell myself I need to take a walk and get some fresh strategy, God speaks with a renewed perspective and enables me to see my place of struggle in a different way. And because the middle is often complex, it also helps us to see the simplicity of goodness around us. We don't need extravagant; we just need the good in a simple form. Little things become the big things when looking for them. It's the text from a friend, the unexpected song that comes through our headphones, the uninterrupted night's sleep that often seems elusive, and the conversation we have with our spouse. It's okay to tell God you need some encouragement, and as you talk with Him, start looking for the way He's answering your prayer.

But the middle *is* closer to the end than we were in the beginning. We are making progress. We will finish. We may need a break, a new strategy, or time for reflection/celebration. But we don't need to give up. In all the places where I've managed to stick with a dream or goal, I'm not disappointed that I stuck it out. Instead, I'm thankful I persevered—even when I doubted myself, was sure I was incapable, and had talked myself out of the reasons why I started.

My son, Bryce, has always enjoyed sports. He has instinctive ability, is competitive, and athleticism seems easy for him. He is fueled by conquering a new challenge. He played football, basketball, soccer, and lacrosse when he was a kid. But now, as an adult, you'll find him hitting the slopes (snowboarding) whenever possible. After a challenging year rehabbing his injury, I wanted to take him to Vermont so he could snowboard on higher-caliber slopes than what we find in central Pennsylvania. I planned a long weekend away, just the two of us, and signed myself up for a ski rental package. I had zero ski experience, aside from one time I went skiing in high school, but it was a disaster and shouldn't count. We drove to Vermont on a Thursday and picked up our ski lift tickets first thing Friday morning. Since it was one of the first weekends the slopes were open for the season, there weren't classes for beginners like me. I thought I could learn the basics from a few YouTube videos and figure it out on the practice slope. Bryce gave me some tips he had learned while watching his friends ski alongside him. And yes, I feel you shaking your head. You know this was a bad idea, even if I hadn't discovered it yet.

My first challenge was the ski lift. Bryce rode along and coached me on my first few rides up the chair lift so I wouldn't fall flat on my face and embarrass myself in front of the entire ski resort (I mean, that was my fear). He helped me make it down the practice course a few times until I felt comfortable and confident in my ability to stop at the bottom without running over anyone. Then I sent Bryce off to snowboard and planned to check in with him later. We spent the day on the slopes, with me on the practice hill, before finishing around 4:00 p.m. The second day was like the first—more practice for me and more time on an actual course for Bryce. I was picking up speed on the practice slope and had a goal of skiing down a real trail before the day ended since it was our final day on the mountain. Around 11:00 a.m., I figured

I knew enough to make it down the mountain, that I was never going to feel ready, and I should go for it.

    I told my son I was ready to take on a real challenge with him. We got in line for the ski lift, but only half of the trails were open, and while our options were limited, I figured the lowest level course must be appropriate for beginners like me. I was wrong. We jumped on the chair lift and began our ascent up the mountain. The climb was much longer than it seemed from the bottom. I was starting to rethink this scenario, but now I was stuck. By the time we finally reached the top, I was sure this was the worst idea I'd ever had, and I would probably die. I told my son there was no way I could ski down this mountain and asked if I could just ride the chair lift back down. He looked at me like I had obviously lost my mind. I looked for a sign offering a backup plan or easy exit, but there wasn't one.

    Bryce told me I could do this and assured me we would do it together. I was starting to believe him until I looked at the first part of the course—there was an almost seven-foot steep downhill section, followed by a sharp curve to the left. If you didn't make the curve, you'd go straight off the side of the mountain. I slowly maneuvered the first section, took a break off to the side of the course, and gathered my courage for the next section. It was straight, with a slight decline, but nothing as intense as the first part. I told myself it was less steep than the practice hill so I would be fine. I figured I should stay close to the far-left side of the course, so I was out of the way of the more experienced skiers and snowboarders. However, I didn't realize the snow on the side was icier. I couldn't control my skis, and it wasn't long until I lost my balance and went sprawling across the course. One ski snapped off while the other remained attached to my boot. I struggled to stand up in the icy snow. It didn't help that I was balancing on one ski. My son grabbed the loose ski and brought it over to me, helped me stand up, and let me balance on him while I reattached. I told him he should go ahead without me. I knew it would take an eternity to get myself down the course, and I didn't want him to waste his time on the slopes. He declined and reinforced his initial commitment—we would do it together.

There were sections where I skied, some where I fell, and others where I snapped off the skis and walked. One of those walking sections came in the middle. It was much like the start—eight feet almost straight down, followed by a sharp curve and another intense decline. At this point, I thought maybe I would walk the rest of the way—I was ready to give up. But Bryce wouldn't let me quit. He told me I could ski the rest of the course, and this was the last time I was walking. I was going to ski the rest of the way.

It was the first time in his life he had been so stern with me. And I knew I had no choice but to listen to him. I was scared, I wanted to take the "easy way out" by walking, but I also didn't want to miss the fun of this experience. The view was incredible—if nothing else, it was providing an impressive story to tell my family later. I didn't want Bryce to always think about the trip and remember I walked the whole way down the mountain. I couldn't see the end of the course, and I wasn't sure what the rest looked like, but I chose to trust Bryce and listen to his voice. He coached me the rest of the way down, patiently going my speed so he could stay right beside me. He was telling me when to lean when to slow down—reminding me not to give up on myself. His words always came when I needed them. It was hard, but we made it.

I realized I wasn't the only novice struggling to navigate the course successfully. By the time we reached the bottom third of the trail, I felt more confident than I had during the prior two-thirds. Some of this confidence was due to the experience I gained navigating the mountain, some came because I could finally see the bottom and I knew it was almost over, but most of the confidence was due to Bryce. I couldn't have made it without him. I would have given up in the middle, or maybe even at the beginning, and asked to ride the lift back down. And had I taken either of those options, I would have missed out on the fun amid the chaos. I gained an opportunity to see Bryce's strengths in a new way and the ability to find a type of determination inside of me I didn't know existed.

My son was exceedingly patient, but he pushed me further than I would have gone on my own. He saw my limitations and knew I didn't have the necessary skill set, but he didn't allow me to give up. And often, when we're stuck in the middle and want to quit, that is exactly the type of encouragement we need. We need someone right beside us who won't let us give up—someone who demands we dig deep and won't quit even when we've convinced ourselves it's the only option. I'm grateful for the way he coached me. I could see the way all the years of team-based sports practices had impacted him. He was a good team player, but he was also an insightful coach.

> We're not alone. Jesus walks with us, and He whispers wisdom and insight. He is cheering us on, especially in the middle.

It's okay to need help. It takes courage to admit we can't do it alone. When we're stuck in the middle, we need someone who understands the path in front of us, will push us out of our comfort zone, and genuinely wants to see us succeed. The partnership offered by a mentor or coach is invaluable. But it's better to find one and lay the foundation of the relationship before we're stuck in the middle section. And it's the same for all the tools we've discussed throughout this book. We need them in place before they are necessary. If we wait until a crisis, we won't feel like doing the work to find the support we need. I can think of several experiences where I would have been more likely to make it to the finish line if I had the strategy and wisdom from a "coach" along the way. Coaches keep us accountable and motivated. They help us develop strength and endurance before it's necessary; then, it doesn't seem so daunting when we hit the most challenging part. Finding a coach can be as simple as looking for someone who has already accomplished what we want to do. And often, they would love the opportunity to give someone the inside information they wish they knew before embarking on their journey.

We're not alone. Jesus walks with us, and He whispers wisdom and insight. He is cheering us on, especially in the middle. God has confidence in us to finish the race before us. He doesn't set us up for failure. But it's also wise to find someone to walk with you (like a coach). And if someone tells you Jesus (Scripture or any element of religious faith) is all you need and throws doubt upon your relationship with God because you're seeking out another dimension of support, it's time to decide whether they belong in your life. We need each other. When God created Adam, He brought him a partner in Eve.

And the truth is, we benefit from wise counsel, such as counselors, coaches, mentors, and pastors. Yes, it's important to memorize Scripture, but statements of faith aren't the only means by which God works. He works through relationships. And there is almost nothing like the miraculous transformation that happens when someone says, "I know what you're going through, I've been there too. Let me help you." Simply knowing we aren't alone, that someone sees us, and they have walked this path too is monumental. And as we make it through the middle and find ourselves at the finish line, we can go back and help others like us who are also stuck in the middle. Who knows, one day, I might become a ski coach who rescues middle-aged women struggling to navigate the mountain.

Chapter 11
Resilience and Determination

In a dream world, all our goals, plans, and pursuits would unfold before us with only momentary delays and slight inconveniences. But that's not the way life works. Yes, you will feel inspiration, reminders of why you're doing this, and the undeniable belief deep inside that this is the place you're supposed to be. But those won't happen every day. Some days you'll be your worst enemy, choosing distraction and self-sabotage instead of pursuing your goal. We will come up against days when we struggle, and that's where resilience and flexibility come in.

Resilience says, "I will bounce back, and make lemonade out of these lemons." We determine our attitude, even if our circumstances are trying to dictate our perspective. And I know it's difficult not to lean in and agree when difficulties seem to pound us like a succession of violent waves. But we can decide we will not be tossed around by those waves this time.

It's hard to make the decision to think, believe, and act in a way that moves us forward when everything inside is screaming, "Go back to bed, pull up the covers, get cozy, and binge your favorite series on Netflix. The heck with today." But avoiding our reality won't make it any better. We transform it one choice at a time. One minute at a time. One deep breath at a time. Even on rainy Mondays in January.

Resilience is our ability to bounce back, to take less-than-stellar circumstances and infuse them with hope and possibility. Self-doubt and accusations won't silence us; instead, we use them as a springboard to launch us higher than we could've gone otherwise. Resilience chooses not to listen to circumstances. It says, "I don't care how often I fall (or am pushed down). I will always rise again. And each time I get back up, I'll do so from even deeper convictions." Every time we use a muscle, we strengthen it, and resilience works the same way.

I've seen this type of impact in my life. As the Amish schoolhouse shooting unfolded, I had a choice. What would I choose to believe about my life? In the very early moments after my initial conversation with the police detectives, I felt God challenge me to choose. And I only had two choices. I could either believe our lives were over, and we were going down like the fastest sinking ship, or I could believe God is everything He says He is and, somehow, He would rescue my family. It's not that I was a giant of faith, but I knew I had nothing to lose by trusting God.

I closed my eyes and prayed, "God, I know the enemy thinks he won today, I know he thinks he won in the schoolhouse, but he has not won here. This will not be the day my kids look back upon and say our lives were over. Yes, this will be a very hard day, and undoubtedly it will be a very difficult season. But God, I believe we will be victorious because of who You are. Whatever You can do with this, do it!"

I wanted healing for my children, and more than ever before, I was committed to being the mom I always wanted to be, one who would create a bright future based on hope and possibility. But if I wanted them to grow in the knowledge and understanding required to do those things, I had to model it for them. I had to invite them into a place where their life story did not define them, and they could develop the courage necessary to create the life they wanted to live.

Resilience is work, but it's worth it. Sometimes we feel the inspiration of resilience when we hear perfectly timed lyrics blasting through our favorite song. But most of the time, it comes because we decided to execute it. We're digging our nails in, pulling ourselves up the mountain, we may be struggling to find the footing necessary for the next upward push, but we're climbing anyway. We are relentless in our pursuit. It doesn't matter how hard it gets or who tells us to give up. We won't quit.

I often think about the prayer I prayed on October 2, 2006. I don't think I needed to give God permission to do what He planned in my life, but I needed to speak those words so I would look for Him. Hope in God was the basis for my perspective, but I layered it with determination to do what was necessary and resilience to believe our life wasn't over. And while all of this is true, I want you to know I'm not perfect. I haven't been a perfect mother. We're all in the same scenario—doing our best with what we've got. And, friend, that's all you must do. It's all God asks of us. Just do the best you can today, right now, in this moment. We're not pursuing perfection. Instead, we're pursuing progress. You can decide today that no matter what your circumstances (or other people) try to tell you, you're not backing down. You're going to stick it out.

And if you're starting with an almost nonexistent level of resilience, it's okay. Remember, resilience is like any other muscle. The more you use it, the stronger it will become. There are a variety of ways to increase our resilience outside of practicing it. Here are a few options:

- Develop a dependable support system.
- View change as a positive force.

- Look at life from an optimistic perspective.
- Become a problem-solver.
- Identify your purpose.
- Create goals.
- Commit to your action steps.

I hope you feel encouraged and empowered as you read the list, because each step you've taken through this book has led you to this point. You have already strengthened your capacity to embrace resilience. You're ready because we've already worked through these concepts. In addition, many of these strategies partner together. For example, if you've identified your purpose, it's easier to create goals. When you know your goals, you can break them down into daily action steps. When we look at life with an optimistic perspective, we are more inclined to seek solutions for our problems instead of merely complaining about them. You can execute resilience not because you have practiced a few skills, but because you can stack the systems together. You are strong. You have the tools, you can do this, and I believe in you. It's time you choose to believe in yourself. It is your life. Live it! You're strong enough to not allow circumstances or someone's misplaced criticism to stop you from doing what you want to do. Nothing worthwhile is easy, but it's worth it.

I'm sure you've heard the quote that says you become like the five people you spend the most time with, or "show me your friends and I'll show you your future." It's true, our friends influence our belief system. If you're thinking about the tools you need for resilience and realize your friends are generally pessimistic, it's time for some new people. I'm not saying you should get rid of all your friends and start over, but consider adding in some friends who embody the characteristics you want for your life. Look for others who know and pursue their goals. Find the ones that are problem-solvers who embrace change and have an optimistic perspective. Cultivate friendships with those who will help you become a better version of yourself.

My resilience and determination exist due to more than just my positive mental outlook, problem-solving ability, or strong support system. It exists because of Jesus. He never fails. When I look across the landscape of my life, yes, I see pain and suffering, but I see His faithfulness. While I wouldn't have purposefully chosen most of my circumstances, I love what God has done with them. I authentically love my life.

> *I can embrace resilience because God has a track record. He has shown up and exceeded my expectations in countless ways throughout our history.*

A few weeks ago, my mom and I talked about how long it's been since my first daughter, Elise, was born—almost twenty-five years. The number carries a more significant impact this year. It's been a quarter-century since the day she was born and died. My mom said sometimes she wonders what Elise would be like had she lived. Would she have gotten married and wanted a family? How would her personality be similar or different from her siblings? She said she couldn't imagine how it felt for me to think about those questions. And yes, it is painful, but there's another side to it. Without losing Elise, which led to my loss of Charlie, I wouldn't have Dan or his family. I wouldn't have my adopted son, Lungelo. And while I wouldn't have chosen the suffering inflicted by Charlie's choices, I can't imagine not living this life.

I can embrace resilience because God has a track record. He has shown up and exceeded my expectations in countless ways throughout our history. If He could take the destruction of 2006 and create a beautiful and fulfilling future with those lifeless pieces, He can do anything. But knowing this doesn't make everything easy. I don't view life as a comparison between the past hardship I experienced and places of current pain. Pain is pain, it's not a competition, and the hard things I've endured since 2006 do not feel less painful based on the tragedy of the Amish schoolhouse shooting. Life and loss don't work that way. We aren't immune to future pain based on past pain. We still feel it deeply. But we can remind ourselves of what God has done in our past, which enables us to embrace resilience and determination for our current moment and all future days.

But the hard part about being an adult is no one will convince you to embrace resilience, work on your mindset, or pursue your goals. Someone else may suggest it, but we must choose it. We are responsible for ourselves and our level of motivation. Resilience is a choice. And it comes more naturally some days versus others. And maybe you're reading this thinking it sounds like a grand theory that won't work for you. You don't feel like being resilient and nothing I say will make a difference. Please know I've felt the same way. The strategies I've shared throughout this book have come through personal development. They aren't merely things I've read and thought sounded like a good idea. I've learned these things the hard way, and often I had to go through them more than once. There are days when I don't feel like doing the work either. And sometimes, I choose the least productive choice—I wallow in my emotions and inactivity. In these times, I know what I'm doing, and I decide to stay there.

When I don't feel like embracing resilience or determination, here's what it comes down to—I have a choice. Do I want to stay stuck, or do I want to move forward? And yes, of course, there are days when I choose to stay stuck. But here's what I know: I will remain in this place until I do something about it. So if I stay stuck today, I will most likely be there tomorrow, the next day, and every day after until I make the change. I must ask myself if I want to stay in this place. Of course not. But am I willing to do the work to move forward?

When I'm not, I coach myself. Why don't I feel like doing the work to move forward? Most of the time, the answer revolves around frustration. Then I ask myself why I'm frustrated (this is the perfect time to grab a journal and walk through the steps with me). Once I've written down why I'm feeling frustrated, I then determine my responsibility in the context of the situation. I invite God into this process and work through the following three questions:

1. What part of this is my responsibility?
2. What part of this is not my responsibility?
3. Where do I need to make a change?

Here's the way this often plays out for me. Why am I feeling frustrated? I'm frustrated because I'm constantly taking care of everyone and never have time for myself. Once I understand the feelings behind my frustration, I work through the questions.

1. What part of this is my responsibility? Have I taken on responsibilities for others instead of allowing them to do it for themselves? Usually, the answer is yes. And then I feel resentful I'm doing things that shouldn't be my responsibility. But they have no idea I feel stressed because they never asked me to do these things.
2. What isn't my responsibility? There are often little things that turn into big frustrations. I need to scale back on the things I'm doing for others.
3. Where do I need to make a change? When asked to do something for someone who can (and should) do it for themselves, I must help them take responsibility. I can offer to assist if they feel stuck or need clarification. But I must prioritize my time and guard my schedule, so I do

not cause additional stress. I need space for self-care and my projects that often end up at the bottom of the list. I can start by blocking off two thirty-minute periods during the week where I read, practice art/mindfulness, or guided imagery meditation. During those times, I'm unavailable for anything else.

Many women don't grow up with role models demonstrating the importance of self-care. And it's not our mom's fault, because no one showed them. We live in a culture that glorifies stress and hustling harder. We feel like we're never doing enough. Our societal role models reinforce this perspective, telling us we can successfully juggle a career, a supposedly happy marriage, and motherhood. We feel the pressure to cultivate Instagram-worthy moments with our kids, dinners rivaling Pinterest photos, and birthday celebrations exceeding the ones we struggled to create in previous years. And then there are Christmas letters we receive detailing all the highs our friends and family have experienced over the past twelve months. We can't keep up, and we tell ourselves we're failing because we can't manage to do the things others seem to accomplish effortlessly.

We are responsible for ourselves and our level of motivation. Resilience is a choice.

But our role models aren't telling the whole story. Their marriages are falling apart, their kids won't spend time with them, and while they sincerely want the story they portray online, it isn't true. They are drowning in pressure and stress, just like us. Very few people have everything together 100 percent of the time. At any moment, we're all about one inch away from losing everything society tells us to manage simultaneously. So if you're feeling burnout, you're not the only one. And the only way we can recover from burnout is to intentionally scale back our self-imposed to-do list and subsequent stress level. We eliminate our ability to engage in resilience when operating from a deficit. When I try to talk myself into resilience but meet repetitive resistance, it is a signal that what I'm feeling is more than everyday stress—it's burnout.

We talked about burnout a few chapters back, but it's worth discussing the application here. Burnout occurs when we've experienced excessive and prolonged stress. We often think of it as related to one's job, but it can happen due to emotional, mental, and physical strain. When we experience burnout, we feel we can't keep up with life's pace or demands. To recover from burnout, we must implement strategies to help us identify and alleviate our stressors. We must also create preventative habits to avoid future setbacks. We can start by identifying the situation responsible for our stress. Once identified, we can change our perception of this scenario and create healthy boundaries. If I'm working too many hours and bringing work home in the evening and on weekends, I must first talk to my supervisor to discuss their expectations versus my self-imposed demands. While it's possible that job stress occurs because the demands are too great for the time frame, I may have an incorrect interpretation of their expectations. Working through this outcome, I can establish boundaries within my role, mindset, or both areas. We heal from burnout through various mechanisms, including positive relationships such as our support system (including counselors), exercise, stress management techniques, and a concentration on self-care.

One of the biggest hurdles is choosing to speak up for ourselves. For me, it's always easier to advocate for someone else versus myself. But we are just as important as anyone else, and we deserve to enjoy our lives. God didn't place us on this earth to dread each day. He didn't create us to exist amid unsurmountable pressure and unending tasks, feeling like Cinderella, constantly putting ourselves at the bottom of the list and waiting for someone to rescue us. We must embrace the fact that we are our fairy godmother. While we all want help from an outside source, and we often wait for someone to notice the unjust nature of our circumstances, the reality is no one is coming. (Because they're so weighed down by their stress, they didn't notice ours.) But there is freedom found in knowing we don't have to wait for someone to rescue us. We can rescue our situation and partner with God to transform it.

And if standing up for yourself still feels too hard, think about it this way. Here is what I tell myself (and my coaching clients) when self-advocacy is a struggle. By helping someone realize the way they are treating you is unacceptable, you're also advocating for their future relationships. You will save someone else from a similar experience by talking about how you feel.

As you embrace resilience, don't discount the impact of conversations with your support system and time spent talking with God. A powerful transformation happens as we say what's on our heart. The conversation may start like most of the psalms David wrote. It's okay to begin by expressing our frustration, detailing our problems, and embracing vulnerability. But then, we remind ourselves of previous places where we overcame trials. We remember when God intervened on our behalf, moments when we didn't see Him coming, but He showed up anyway and changed everything. As we stand on the pronouncement of past miracles, we are inspired to believe they will happen again. We believe in God's partnership and our ability to overcome. It is exactly what happened to David.

Resilience comes as we embrace the courage necessary to make the changes we wish someone would make for us. We become our fairy godmother because we finally understand we're not doing it alone. We have friends cheering us on, speaking hope and belief over us for as long as it takes. And we have God. We're standing firm, believing He will make a way, even when we can't see it. We are not a victim of our circumstances. Instead, we are victorious.

We hold power to make that choice. And we must decide; we can't simply say we're not choosing. Not making a choice is still a choice. It's okay to pause, reflect, research, and recover. But then we jump back in and pursue the life God designed us to live. The fulfillment that comes from finding, pursuing, and doing this thing within our hearts is powerful.

Chapter 12
Defying Limitations

In almost any pursuit, we reach the point where we've gone as far as we believe is possible. But this doesn't mean we've reached an actual barrier to progress. Most often, the limitation exists within our mind. When we say, "This is as far as I can go," we aren't inferring it's as far as humanly possible. Instead, it's as far as we believe *we* can go. If I think about all the places in life where I've declared a limit, it comes at the end of my resources, physical stamina, and mental ability. It sounds like this: I don't want to spend any more than this; I'm at my limit. I'm exhausted, and I have reached my limit. I can't deal with any more of your attitude; I've reached my limit! There is a threshold in each of these places I will not cross.

So then, if we think about it based on an idea, goal, or plan, when we say there is a limitation, we are wrong. It's not that we *can't* do it. We do not need more resources to accomplish it or a greater level of stamina to keep up with it. Our perspective comes because we don't know *how* to do it. We mean, "I've reached the limit of my capacity, and I need help to move forward." But if we're going to acknowledge our limitations and recognize we need help, there is a place of vulnerability we must be willing to embrace. When I think about my life, the times I believed I had reached my limit were places where I couldn't embrace the level of vulnerability necessary to ask for help.

The inability to ask for help is often a trauma response. We think we should be able to handle it on our own. We see the struggle others are having around us, and we don't want to burden them, so we don't ask for their help. All the while, we feel like we're drowning inside, and we know we can't do this alone. It was especially true for me after the Amish schoolhouse shooting. My parents were wonderful, but I knew they were dealing with their sense of loss and devastation. So I was careful in what I asked of them. I didn't want to complicate their healing process. But it further reinforced my belief that I shouldn't ask for help.

It has also been one of the more significant areas of struggle in my marriage to Dan. He authentically wants me to ask for help, and while I'm better at it than I was in 2007 when we got married, it's still not easy. In the beginning, when I asked for help, I had to remind myself our relationship was dependable—I could trust Dan wanted to help me and asking him wasn't placing an additional burden on him. I grew in my ability to ask because he came through. I could look back at past experiences where I asked for help and received what I thought I needed. But it doesn't always work that way, sometimes the way Dan responds to my request for help is different from what I expected. In those moments I must remind myself he is doing his best and I can trust him.

As I've grown in my ability to ask for help, it's strengthened my desire to self-advocate. Everything I've shared with you works together, and when used well, these concepts become layers which fit perfectly. But it also means when I struggle in one area, it impacts another. If I struggle to ask for help, then I'm less likely to self-advocate. My inability to self-advocate connects to a lack of self-worth. As I allow God to re-create the foundation of my identity in Him, I find my value, which gives me the confidence to self-advocate, and then enables me to ask for help.

If our capacity limits are self-determined, then it's worth asking ourselves, "Why do I believe this is a limitation?" In terms of finances, it's an easy answer. There is a limited amount of money available. But how do we define our limitations regarding mental, emotional, or physical endurance or abilities? Our limits often come from the negative self-talk we've allowed and the negative voice around us. When we tell ourselves we have hit our limit, the truth is we are saying we don't want to do more. And as we've discussed before, our perspective becomes our reality. But we're already working on the negative self-talk. We're replacing it with positive statements grounded in truth. We are embracing the grace to make progress without expecting perfection. Instead of ruling our actions based on success or failure, we're identifying strategies that worked and replacing the ones that didn't yield the desired outcome.

The inability to ask for help is often a trauma response.

Asking for help doesn't mean we are weak or incapable. It's not an indicator of failure, but many of us have interpreted it as such. It's not that we don't trust someone enough to ask for help, but we (consciously or unconsciously) feel like we should not need help. We believe we should possess the skills or ability to handle everything and not have to ask. So we don't ask for help from those around us, and we don't ask God to help us. We've learned, intentionally or otherwise, to be self-sufficient. And then we start to feel resentful because no one is helping us, including God.

This problem is better addressed, like everything else—objectively. And the only way to overcome it is by changing our narrative and thinking about our self-imposed expectations. When I realize I won't ask for help because I don't want to appear weak,

I think about it as if this scenario applied to a friend or one of my kids. It's easy for me to lay it out as if it were one of my kids because we've had these conversations. It generally begins with me noticing something is bothering them. When I ask what is going on, they mention a specific scenario I could help them overcome; it's outside their ability level. My response is always, "I wish you would've asked sooner. I can help with that; we can do it together. You don't need to struggle under the weight of it alone." They look relieved and then say, "Well I didn't want to ask you, I mean, I should be able to do this on my own."

While allowing my kids to struggle through typical life challenges is essential, it's okay for them to need my help. Overcoming struggles cultivates self-confidence and resourcefulness. We often discover skills and abilities through challenges, but there is a blessing in knowing you're not alone. As a parent, I want my kids to understand they can count on me not to come to their rescue but to help them when they need me. And I think God wants the same for us. There are many things I can handle, but there are days when I struggle mentally, emotionally, and physically. Sometimes I don't want to do what's asked of me. And I feel this way even though I know God infuses me with strength when I feel weak. When I'm exhausted, He's not telling me to dig deeper or try harder. He's not a drill sergeant. He is a loving father who walks with me. God does not despise my cries for help. It's the opposite; He *wants* me to ask Him. When I ask, it shows I trust Him, recognize I need Him, and am willing to lean into our relationship.

Similarly, my husband wants me to ask for help, and he appreciates when I embrace the vulnerability necessary to ask. Asking demonstrates my trust in him. I see his help as valuable because he is valuable. He doesn't want to be my last resort. If I tried everything else, and only asked for help when nothing else worked, I would undermine his value in my life. My inability to ask would hurt him. And I wouldn't want to be someone's last resort either. I wouldn't want my kids, husband, family, or friends to feel like they could only ask me to help them if they had exhausted all other options and had no choice.

God doesn't want to be our last resort either. He wants to be our first call. Who is the person you reach out to first? Who is the one you instinctively go to when you need help—a listening ear, wisdom, strategies, or physical assistance with a task? This person has cultivated a meaningful relationship with you. You know they're not going to make you feel bad for asking. They aren't going to go through a checklist of other options you should have used before calling them. They will invest themselves in you because they care about you. God wants that spot in our lives. He loves us more than we will ever understand. His love is deeper and more constant than any person we will ever know. He is always present, never too busy, and never distracted. We are not an inconvenience—we are His first choice.

We often discover skills and abilities through challenges, but there is a blessing in knowing you're not alone.

Maybe it's hard for you because you've reached out to friends or family members before, and instead of receiving help, you ended up with discouragement. But maybe in the complexity of why it's hard for you to ask for help, it's not just about embracing vulnerability and overcoming the fear of looking incapable if we ask. It hurts when we trust another person with our vulnerability and acknowledgment we need them, only to find they have no desire to help us. We feel the sting of pain, and it lingers. If their words were negative, we replay them over and over in our minds. We started to believe them even if what they spoke was not valid.

Why are some people so negative? Why do they ruin our plans and destroy our dreams? Is it because they see us as weak or incapable? I've asked myself these questions, and you probably have too. And friend, based on personal experience, I don't think it has anything to do with us. It's all about them. Their negative (and hurtful) statements come from their place of insecurity and jealousy. If you need proof, think about something you've thought or said when scrolling through social media. You see a friend embarking on a new career, ministry opportunity, or social cause, and what's the first thing that pops into your head? If it's always something like, "I'm so happy for her!" Then you are a much better person than I am. Sometimes I see these things and say, "Wow, good for her, must be nice." I am harsh because I am jealous and insecure.

My insecurity and jealousy have nothing to do with the other person; it has everything to do with me. I embrace insecurity when I've forgotten (or become disconnected from) my value. Instead of criticizing someone else, I need to spend time with God. I find renewal as He defines my worth. I must choose to believe His words and cement them deep inside my heart. And sometimes, my criticism comes not from a lack of value but jealousy over another's experiences or accomplishments. I'm sure we've all scrolled through social media and felt a tinge of jealousy when we saw a friend post pictures of a fabulous vacation, date night with their spouse, or quality time spent with friends. We start to think about how long it's been since we felt the joy of a similar experience and jealousy creeps in. It's easier not to do this when I have a relationship with the individual. When a close friend posts pictures of her most recent Disney trip, I view them in light of her everyday life. I know her struggles. I remember the conversation when she talked about how badly her family needed a vacation. She said they were limping to the finish line of their work week, trying desperately to hold it all together. I view her photos with compassion for her struggle and celebrate the happiness she cultivated amid stress and uncertainty. I don't feel jealous when I look at her pictures because I know she more than deserved these moments.

But most of our "friends" on Facebook or Instagram are little more than acquaintances. We don't rub shoulders, share struggles over a cup of coffee, or walk in the authenticity of our day-to-day lives. All we see are their highlight reels because they're trying to protect their family. They don't want everyone to know their pain. They know one day their kids will look back at this season, and they don't want them to read about how much their mom struggled, the way she doubted herself daily, or felt uncertain they would survive the season.

Social media isn't the best place for us to find support for our brokenness or vent about our family. We all have struggles; and somehow, we forget this truth when watching the highlights go by. We imagine these other women only know the good stuff, the moments that seem to slip through our fingers or only exist in our dreams. We tell ourselves we're the only ones worried our kids are vaping, smoking marijuana, sending nude pictures, and having sex. So, we see the summer trips and weekends away, and we are jealous because we're stuck in the middle of all the hard things instead of experiencing the bliss of an escape from it all. But the reality is our friends posting those photos know the same struggles we know. And instead of feeling jealous that they got something we desperately want, we can choose to celebrate them and pull inspiration from their lives. We can also be the one who celebrates them in their middle section, just as we wish someone would do for us. Because if we knew the valley they were walking through, we wouldn't feel jealous. We wouldn't want their good stuff because it came with all the brokenness they've faced behind closed doors.

We define self-imposed limits as we see the disparity between what's happening in ourselves and those around us. We get to choose the voices we listen to, the ones we dismiss, and the ones we overhaul. And we must choose because, too often, we allow everything to exist in our heads and become truths in our hearts without questioning whether it belongs there. Some of us experienced the ridicule of classmates, teachers, or family members when we were going up. For many, the voice of self-doubt and condemnation initially came decades ago, when we were too young to realize it didn't belong or know how to do something about it. While it is essential to have the type of people in our lives we can trust to tell us the truth, and not only the things we want to hear, it is also imperative these people genuinely have our best in mind. I am willing to accept criticism from someone who wants to help me become a better version of myself and invest in the process. I've learned (the hard way) not to accept criticism from those who want to nail me to the wall and walk away.

Unfortunately, this scenario has played out in my life on more than one occasion. And it's hard to understand why the very people who should invest in our lives (or even say they will) want nothing more than to condemn us and leave. They know us well enough to identify our sensitivities and weaknesses and use them to their advantage. There is almost nothing worse than the realization that comes when you've given a place of authority to someone who only wants to wound you.

When this happens, and as we see the reality of the relationships around us, we must protect ourselves, our self-worth, and create boundaries. And not only do we often have to physically remove them from our world, but we also have to kick them out of our heads. I still remember specific conversations where those I trusted condemned me. I can picture where we sat, the way I opened my heart, and the stunning realization when they nailed me to the wall and walked away. I don't think I'll ever forget those moments, but I see them differently now. At the time, I thought I was the problem, but in the years since, I began to realize they were wrong. My dad helped me gain clarity after one of these conversations. He called me a few hours after and could tell by the sound of my voice something was wrong. He asked why I was upset. I told him about the conversation. I knew I had forever lost a close friend.

As we talked, he helped me realize a more profound truth than what I saw on the surface. My dad saw it objectively and helped me do the same. I am grateful for his perfectly timed phone call, his willingness to enter my brokenness, and the way he helped me see a deeper reality. His instinct, perception, and compassionate heart are some of the things I miss most about him. We all need someone in our lives like my father. We need someone to talk to when we have hard conversations and feel condemned by someone we trust. We need someone who can help us sort it out and decide what is true and what is a lie. I'm grateful God has placed other friends in my life who will listen and give this type of feedback.

In addition to finding it in another person, we can hear it from God. He knows our hearts and the heart of every other person on this earth. He will bring clarity and help us to redefine our limitations. Our perception of a limit generally exists because the limit is as far as we've gone before. But the past doesn't have to be our future. God never stops creating. He is creating within us and throughout the world. He redefines our past experiences. While we may not know or perceive we can reach further than we have in the past, God has new ways for us to approach challenging situations. He inspires a shift in perspective which makes the seemingly impossible possible.

Chapter 13
Before and After

I'm not the same person I was before I knew pain. It changed me. It changed the way I see the world around me and the way I see myself. And much of the shift came because I now see my life as a gift. But before October 2006, this wasn't my perspective. It's one of the things that changed through losing my first husband. Although I felt devastated about my circumstances, in some ways, moving forward, I had the opportunity to create the life I wanted. I had a second chance. I realized each day is a gift, and through seemingly ordinary moments, God offers opportunities. In the past, when I felt inspired by a new idea, I questioned God repeatedly. Even when I was sure He was speaking, I still asked Him to confirm. I wanted to see it on a billboard, painted across the sky, or written on a fortune cookie because I wasn't 100 percent certain. And it came from a good place. I wanted to honor Him. I wanted to make the right choice but staying in a position of uncertainty was paralyzing. All I did was question Him. I couldn't move forward because I wasn't sure. And I can't imagine how many times God tried to give me another beautifully crafted opportunity, but I refused it, because, what if I got it wrong?

While I've been intentionally working on correcting my perspective over the last fifteen years, the most significant change has occurred in the previous three years, during the pandemic, while I was in college. I didn't go to college after high school—I got married, and you know the rest of the story. As an adult, I hadn't given college much thought. And by 2019, I had three kids in college, so I wasn't thinking about it for myself. But in the final week of 2019, I began asking God what He had for me in 2020. My exact words were, "God, what do You have for me in 2020? I don't want to miss it." I knew I had missed out on things He had tried to give me before, and I was not going to do it again in the coming year. I also needed a keystone goal. I was ready for the challenge of a big project. On New Year's Eve at 6:30 p.m., I felt God's answer as I was in the car heading out to meet friends for dinner. He spoke one word, "College." My immediate response was, "God, You're crazy. I can't go to college. I have three kids in college!" But I held on to His words and continued to think about what He might have in store for me. A few weeks before, I had helped my son choose classes for the spring semester. I remember browsing the university's psychology course catalog and thinking I wanted to take some of those classes. But as God spoke a new opportunity, I shrank back from His gift.

I kept the conversation to myself until January 10, 2020. Then I told my husband what happened during our drive to meet friends for dinner on New Year's Eve. He thought it was a great idea—and of course, he would. He always supports my big projects. He started telling me how smart I was, how well I would do; he believed I could do anything. I wasn't convinced. But I decided to apply. Either God would open the doors, or He wouldn't. I told God I would follow through on what I felt Him say, but He would have to work it out. When I think back over the past two decades, if there was one phrase I've said most often, it's, "God, I don't know how You'll do this, but I trust You." I didn't know how to balance my speaking schedule, parenting, household responsibilities, and time for Dan. However, I knew God could see it all in a way I couldn't.

And He made it work. Ten days after the conversation with my husband, I began taking classes at Immaculata University—half on campus and the other half online. I was two months into my studies when the pandemic hit, which cleared my speaking schedule. I had almost no speaking events for the following two years, which created additional time in my schedule. I took five or six classes each semester year-round and finished my degree in thirty months instead of four years. And along the way I discovered strengths, passion, and joy I didn't know existed within me. I think about who I thought I was, or maybe it's better said, who I thought I *wasn't* when I graduated high school. I didn't believe I was intelligent, special, or strong. I didn't think there was anything extraordinary inside of me, and I certainly wouldn't have thought I could withstand the tragedies I've known, blend a family, successfully navigate adoption, graduate college, and find a way to authentically love my life. But I am, and I have, and you can find them too.

I hear you though, the thought of a fast-paced college experience is not on your to-do list, and maybe you're even telling God He better not ask you to go because you'll run the other way. God knows our hearts and sees the treasure deep within. He's aware of our doubts, fears, and secret desires. In His infinite mercy, He uses unexpected paths to lead us to breathtaking destinations. At Immaculata, I met many inspiring professors who instilled courage, deepened my convictions, and helped me create a new season. I am forever grateful for their investment. I couldn't have done this on my own. I needed God's inspiration, my husband's support, and the insight shared by my professors.

I think about my "before and after," and it's overwhelming. There are so many seasons that fit into this framework. God has literally done the impossible, transforming the places I would've deemed "unsalvageable" and written off without his plan of redemption. The comparison between how I saw myself at eighteen years old and now, in my mid-forties, is striking. When I graduated high school, I felt as though I had little value, but now I see my worth, not solely due to the things I have accomplished but who I am inside. Then there's the before and after of motherhood—the devastation I felt after losing my first daughter compared to the gift of mothering six children, including my adopted son. There are also the moments spent in deep sorrow, unable to comprehend why my first husband would choose to inflict devastation on our community versus the ability to step out from under the weight of our brokenness. I am alive, each day is a gift, and there is more to do.

My life contains stunning befores and afters. And I'm not the only one. The Bible conveys stories of others just like me. Their before holds no hope for the after that became their reality. Men like Joseph. His brothers betrayed him and sold him into slavery. His story seems to go from bad to worse as Joseph receives a prison sentence for a crime he didn't commit. And there, within the lonely prison God redeems his devastation. Joseph becomes second in command, interprets Pharaoh's dream, creates (and executes) a plan to save the nation from the impending famine, and witnesses the fulfillment of his childhood dream—his brothers bow down to him. There's no way we would predict the ending of his story based on the context of the beginning or the middle, but God does it anyway. His story shows me that while God always fulfills His promises—sometimes it takes decades—and the road He calls us to walk may seem like it's taking us further and further away from our dreams. But God always gets us to the place of His promise, even if the path doesn't make sense.

We see it in Esther—an orphaned child. She's not the girl you'd pick out as the next queen. But she wins the heart of the king. She becomes queen of a nation, risks her life for her people, unravels the plan to destroy the Jews, and inspires confidence in countless women throughout history. Her story hasn't ended because she continues to shine as a beacon of hope, reminding us it's okay to acknowledge our fear, but we must step into God's call, trusting He is more significant than all we face.

David's story also inspires me. I wouldn't have chosen a young shepherd boy to lead God's kingdom, but God saw something in him most would've missed based on outward assessments. He destroyed the giant who had terrorized communities and annihilated men more formidable than he. But he wasn't perfect. David fell in love with another man's wife, had him killed, and took her for himself. He faced the punishment of disobedience but always kept his heart open to God. And the outcome is God called him a man after His own heart. David never lost his authentic vulnerability. He reminds me God isn't expecting perfection, our sin doesn't disqualify us from God's plan, and my relationship with God leads to daily transformation.

> God always fulfills His promises—sometimes it takes decades—and the road He calls us to walk may seem like it's taking us further and further away from our dreams. But God always gets us to the place of His promise, even if the path doesn't make sense.

It's easy to read through these stories in the Bible or hear someone talk about the restoration God's brought into their lives and think it happened quickly. But redemption is not usually a quick fix. For most of these people, their process spanned decades. And it's the same for us. When we're waiting on God to fulfill a promise, we will often wait longer than we hoped, but we can trust God will not only do what He said but exceed our expectations.

He's good, and He always keeps His promises. I imagine Joseph probably felt forgotten, but I think he, like Esther, and David, told God how he felt. At the end of his story, he tells his brothers they shouldn't feel bad about what they did to him because God used it to save a nation. Joseph meant what he said. He saw how God used his circumstances for something greater than he ever imagined possible. And then he extended the redemption he knew to his siblings. Unless he had allowed God to meet him in his brokenness, bring healing through his pain, and give him eyes to see the story behind his brothers' choices, he could not have authentically desired their healing. If he were bitter and angry over all they had done to him, he wouldn't have been concerned about their healing—instead, he would have wanted to punish them (and rightly so). But instead of punishment, he chose mercy.

When I think about Joseph's before and after, what captivates me isn't merely the circumstances of his life, although they are stunning. But more than circumstance, I'm captivated by his heart and the healing he had to have known. If God can heal a man whose family sold him into slavery, which led to every other painful experience along his journey, God can heal me. And He can heal you too.

And yes, the redemption and restoration cause a shift in our circumstances, but that's not what changes us. My relationship with my husband, Dan, is a beautiful part of the story God's written in my life. But he is not my redemption. He's not my restoration. Restoration and redemption come when we allow God to change something inside us. It's understandable to want external change, and it feels natural to assume circumstantial change would bring a radical transformation inside of us, but redemption isn't based on circumstance. If I had not allowed God to heal the trauma that came with losing my first husband, I would have sabotaged my relationship with Dan. If Joseph had only witnessed the fulfillment of the dream he had when he was seventeen years old (his brothers bowing down) without allowing God to do deep work within his broken heart, his words would have had a different impact. He would have undoubtedly wanted vengeance instead of mercy. Circumstances are not the demonstration of redemption. Redemption lives inside our hearts. It's born there, grows there, and spreads throughout our body, impacting our words and changing the way we see ourselves, and it changes everything. Our before and after aren't the same as a home renovation snapshot or significant weight-loss photos. We probably won't be able to capture the transformation in a photograph. It looks like hope. And without hope, we won't have the capacity to believe in our before and after.

God's ability to walk you through the redemption story He plans for your life requires very little on your part. He's not asking for perfection, prior training, or even confidence. All He asks for is your partnership—your willingness to walk the path, no matter how long it takes or where it takes you. Hope is an indestructible force, seemingly insignificant, not outwardly identifiable, but it is extraordinary. Hope stays when everything inside you wants to run away. Hope believes when circumstances tell you to quit. Hope is patient when our natural inclination is impatience. Hope asks for help. It declares more than we know now and cries out for redemption. God tells us that hope never disappoints. And He should know—He *is* the God of hope. He won't disappoint us. Even if what we're walking through came from someone else's choices. He promises redemption, a life where we know joy even when we've experienced brokenness. These aren't just phrases for a keychain or bumper sticker. They are real because He is real.

And maybe you're feeling a little like the father mentioned in Mark 9. You believe (or you feel an awakening of belief), but still, a part of you is scared to believe. Maybe you're thinking, *What happens if I believe all this and nothing changes? What if I'm disappointed again?* I've told you some of my stories, but I want to share those that have impacted me, like Joseph, Esther, and David. But there's a man mentioned in the Bible (Mark 9:24) I identify with, and I shared a bit of his story a few chapters ago. His honesty captures my attention. He doesn't say what he thinks Jesus wants to hear. Instead, he speaks from the truth deep within him. His child is suffering. Something is happening inside his son, and the father knows without divine intervention, his son will eventually die. I can't imagine the pain this father feels, the agony of never knowing if today will be the day he loses his boy. But I see him, and I see the pain of helplessness. His child needs more than he can give him, but he's heard about this man who heals people. And he decides he's not holding back. This father doesn't wish Jesus would show up for him. Instead, he does whatever it takes to get his son in front of this man. And getting face-to-face with Jesus was not easy. There were crowds, hundreds and thousands of people (depending on the day), and then there were the disciples. Trying to get within sight of Jesus took a miracle, but the father doesn't embrace the excuses—he fights for the blessing. And we get a glimpse of his conversation in Mark 9. He begins by telling Jesus about his son. He says, "If you can do anything, have compassion on us and help us" (Mark 9:22). Jesus responds by repeating the statement in the form of a question, "'If you can'! All things are possible for one who believes" (v. 23). Immediately after Jesus spoke those words the father cries out, "I believe, help my unbelief" (v. 24). His honesty gets my attention every time I read this passage. Here

> *God's ability to walk you through the redemption story He plans for your life requires very little on your part. He's not asking for perfection, prior training, or even confidence. All He asks for is your partnership—your willingness to walk the path, no matter how long it takes or where it takes you.*

was this miracle man, who went around healing people, and He was the only hope this father had for his son. And yet, even amid his hope, he battled his doubts.

I can imagine why he battled. Maybe he had taken his son to countless specialists who seemed hopeful initially but then decided they couldn't help him. Perhaps he had spent every ounce of energy, time, and finances trying to find someone to heal his son. And in each prior experience, when he thought he had finally found the right person, he walked away disappointed and weighed down by his helplessness. I think we've all felt that way. Our reasons are different, but the result is the same. We put our hope in something that seemed perfect, only to discover later there was no redemption coming. And we've learned not to get our hopes up because we don't want to risk disappointment. But even as God asks us to hope, He isn't offended by our doubts. He doesn't shame the father for admitting his unbelief. Jesus doesn't refuse to heal the child because the father doubted.

In the end, Jesus does heal this man's son, but I don't think it's the only healing Jesus performed within the context of this story. When I think about this father, I put myself in his shoes. As a parent, there is almost nothing as profound as someone who steps into our child's lives and gives them something we're incapable of giving. This father, who had carried the weight of his son's condition, was free of the guilt and pain he knew. I can only imagine how his heart soared, watching the healing wash over his child. Jesus answered his cries in an instant. His circumstance changed, but I believe even more profound healing happened inside of him. He knew God loved him and accepted his imperfections instead of holding them against him. God loved him in the authenticity of who he was—period. He didn't have to change his doubts. God changed them.

Hope is a powerful force. It spans both secular and religious communities. Harvard University conducted a study through its

Human Flourishing Program, which included over 13,000 participants with a median age of 66. They discovered "those with more hope throughout their lives had better physical health, better health behaviors, better social support and a longer life."[3] Hope has a tangible impact on life experience, longevity, and mental, physical, and emotional wellness. Hope is our belief in the capacity for positive change, and it has made all the difference in my life. I have hope in who God is and the way He works in my life, but I also have hope in my ability to overcome. I can do hard things because I have the tools to work through them and I'm not alone in them. God comes and sits with me in my pain, speaks life to my brokenness, and pours out His redemption even amid my doubts. He transforms the places of despair, discouragement, and the deadness we feel inside. In His hands, the sorrow of our "befores" become the substance of our celebratory "afters."

> He is filled with eager anticipation for everything He has planned for you. For Him, this is like Christmas morning. He knows you're about to unwrap something that will change everything.

Pain of loss bathes my befores—the loss of my first daughter, second pregnancy, husband, and father—but my afters are different. Compassion for others—eyes that see brokenness and a desire to do something about it—cover them. I couldn't have my afters unless I went through the befores. While I wouldn't have chosen my circumstances, I love what God has done with them. My life is full and rich, due to the inner transformation and the ability to use my pain for good in others. I love who I've become. If I could go back and do it all over again, I would tell myself to embrace this level of hope in every moment of life. If I had embraced hope earlier, I wouldn't have needed so many confirmations when I felt God spoke, and I wouldn't have missed so many beautiful opportunities. I know I wasted what God tried to give me. My doubt was the loudest voice in my head. And while the realization evokes a sting of sadness, I am grateful for the way God has used even those moments.

He doesn't waste anything. Nothing is a coincidence. He is in every moment, each breath, and glimmer of hope. And now it's your turn. It is your invitation to embrace hope, even when you must also acknowledge your doubts. God isn't disappointed by your authenticity; He loves you just the way you are. And He is filled with eager anticipation for everything He has planned for you. For Him, this is like Christmas morning. He knows you're about to unwrap something that will change everything. He's holding this gift out to you. Hope. One small word with a giant impact. It doesn't matter what path you've taken until this moment. What's most important now is that you embrace what He's offering. Your circumstances are not the definition of your life. Instead, the definition comes through your choices. It's the way you stay in the fight, your choice to believe despite the obstacles, your patience as God unfolds His miracle, and your willingness to ask for help. Ask Him to show up; ask for the dream in your heart, the opportunities you've secretly wanted. And don't stop. Hope persists, and it will not disappoint you. Because your hope is not dependent upon your ability to make something out of nothing—it's what God always does.

Chapter 14
Fight for the Blessing

My friend Dawn spoke a sentence over a decade ago that has stuck with me through every season since. Her words come in a whisper when I need them most, "Are you going to settle for the excuse or fight for the blessing?" I'll be honest and admit there have been many times I have settled. I don't always fight. But looking back, I wish I had always fought for the blessing. When I settle, I choose what seems to be the easier option. But it's only easier in the short term. In the long term, the places where I've settled become costly. When I settle, I take the easy way out because I don't want the work associated with fighting for the blessing. Fighting sounds fierce and complicated because I imagine heading into the battle on my own.

We all have places where we settle. Sometimes we feel exhausted. We've focused on our limitations and admitted we don't want the fight, so instead of doing the work, we drop out. This concept is evident when I think about how many times I've attempted to change my diet or develop a regular exercise routine. I might maintain consistency for two weeks, but then something happens, and I quit. Honestly, I can come up with reasons to settle. I don't even need life to create them for me.

We also do this with our mindset. We're stressed or frustrated, so instead of taking a walk or practicing meditation, we grab some chocolate, scroll social media, or pour a glass of wine. And while chocolate, social media, and wine aren't necessarily bad, it's all about the way we use them. Since I brought up alcohol, let's take a minute to talk about it. I don't think God has a problem with alcohol—the first miracle Jesus performs involves Him turning water into wine. If God was anti-alcohol, I think the miracle would have looked different. However, I believe it is meant as part of the celebration, not our therapy. And I say this while admitting I've poured a glass of wine to take the edge off my day. But I know those were settling moments. I was not fighting for any blessing even though it was the better choice. Instead of grabbing the wine, I could have used guided imagery, an art/mindfulness exercise, or meditative prayer. Had I utilized those tools, I would have cultivated a positive internal transformation instead of dulling my frustration. When I utilize the positive practices we've discussed, I lower my stress level, regain composure, and take the edge off my day in a way that lasts. I'm still going to have a glass of wine to celebrate from time to time, but I'm not going to count down my day to a cocktail. The same is true for chocolate. Instead of reaching for a bag of semi-sweet chocolate chips when I'm stressed because it's 4:30 and I have no plan for dinner, I'll challenge my negative self-talk and pencil a reminder in my calendar to meal plan for the week. I can either settle for the excuse (I'm too busy, I'm tired of cooking, it's so much work) or fight for the blessing (healthy meals, family connections at the dinner table, and a reduced stress level because I thought ahead).

This question is always the right question, "Will I settle for the excuses or fight for the blessings?" And it reminds me I always have a choice. Not choosing is still a choice. As a little girl, I loved reading *Choose Your Own Adventure* books, and the one I remember most was *Alice in Wonderland*. The reader controls the outcome as Alice encounters a situation where she must weigh out her options. There were always two choices, and they went something like this, "If you want Alice to go down the rabbit hole, turn to page 7, but if you want Alice to ignore the rabbit and stay on the path, turn to page 21." It looks the same when I face a situation where I either choose to settle or fight for the blessing. "If you want Marie to fight, turn to page 26, but if you want her to settle, turn to page 9." If I saw it like that in print, I'd never choose to settle. I wouldn't choose it for someone else and wouldn't want it for myself. In black and white, settling is a terrible idea. My brain immediately jumps to the negative implication of the decision. Inside, I'm saying, "No, no, no, don't choose to settle; you know nothing good comes of it." And when I settle, I usually end up circling the same mountain. I find myself at a similar decision a few months later, annoyed I wasted time only to find that at some point, I will have to choose to fight.

If I know nothing good comes from settling and inevitably, I'll find myself face-to-face with the same decision later, why do I still choose it? I decide to settle because I'm human, listen to the negative voice in my head, and expect the worst outcome (thank you, trauma-based perspective). Most of the time, I don't want the result associated with settling, but I fear it less than I fear that fighting will lead to failure. It's one thing to choose to settle and know what's coming. But it's another thing to decide to fight only to face disappointment and the perception of a failed outcome. Settling is safe. Fighting is risky.

When I settle, I guarantee myself a specific, identifiable result. It's comforting. But if we watched our life unfold as the character in a book or our favorite Netflix series, we'd be screaming from the couch, "No, don't do it. Don't settle. You were born for the fight. You can do this, and you have to do it!" But I don't stop to think through the process of choices and outcomes. I roll right on through to my comfort zone. And each time I end up there, I move further and further away from the life God designed. He can bring me back on track, and when I'm ready, He will. But I took myself off course, and fixing it requires time and correction. And I don't mean correction as punishment, but a course correction.

 Think about it like an airplane. If it's flying straight and level, the passengers are comfortable. The flight is enjoyable. They can move around, use the bathroom, and receive drinks/snacks from the flight attendants. But if the pilot discovers they need to change course to avoid a sudden storm or other flight interference, the captain throws on the seatbelt sign, tells everyone to remain seated, and asks the flight attendants to sit down. It can evoke panic in some of the passengers. What seemed comfortable and enjoyable a few moments before, now cause uncertainty and anxiety. The plane encounters turbulence. The pilot begins to turn the aircraft. And while the angle isn't noticeable unless you look out the window, the sight of the world below, now diagonal instead of horizontal, causes concern. The pilot successfully navigates the course correction, and it's not long until everything is back to normal, but you're telling yourself you don't ever want to do that again.

 And it's what I've experienced after I've settled, realized I'm not where I want to be, and felt the correction necessary to get back on track. God's the pilot in this scenario, and I'm the passenger. He knows how to direct my life successfully, but it's not always comfortable, and often I tell myself I don't ever want to do that again. It takes work to turn my plane around, I need to remind myself it's going to be uncomfortable, and I'll have to fight my desire to play it safe during the correction and after. In these moments of correction, I can again choose to settle, and then it becomes a vicious cycle. But I don't think through this when I'm deciding whether to fight or settle. I want what's comfortable, and if I don't intentionally analyze the process, I'll choose immediate comfort, which only leads to future discomfort.

There is another way. I can choose to embrace the fight, which always leads to blessings. Settling leads to discomfort, while fighting leads to a blessing. When I see it all in black and white, the choice is clear—I will fight because I want what comes on the other side. But sometimes, there are doubts inside me that rise through my negative self-talk. They remind me of past attempts and the way they didn't work out. And I don't interject reason and truth into these conversations, they are one-sided, and I allow the negative self-talk to carry it all. The truth is, it didn't work in previous attempts because I chose to settle somewhere along the way when I faced a choice. I'm not incapable and the system didn't fail me. Instead, I stopped trying. But I don't tell the negative voice to sit down and shut up. Instead, I listened to it as though it was the authority figure in my life. And that voice is never going to push me toward the fight.

> *I can trust God to meet me in the hard place, and it's okay if others don't understand. I don't need another's permission to pursue the dreams and goals God births within my heart. I don't need to justify or explain anything. I need to fight for the blessing.*

But I've learned how to correct my negative self-talk. So this time it's different. Even through the process of writing this book, I found myself fighting for the blessing. My internal dialogue sounded like this, *Yes, I know there have been times I've given up. In those moments, I chose to settle. I didn't do the work, but this time I'm doing the work. I'm choosing to fight for the blessing. I know how to set realistic goals. I see the value of celebrating all the small steps, and I'm inviting God into this process. I'm going to dream a new dream and follow it through. I'll embrace resilience, when necessary, defy my self-perceived limits, and keep a perspective rooted in hope. This time is different because I'm different.* And finally, my negative-self talk had nothing to say. It sits there with a smug expression, arms crossed, looking down its nose at me, and I know I have something to prove. But I can do it, and I will.

I remind myself of the times before when I haven't settled. The fights I've chosen, and the blessings I've received. The list is long. After the Amish schoolhouse shooting, I believed God would meet me and redeem my life, but He exceeded my expectations. When others told me I was entering into a relationship with Dan too soon, suggested he was taking advantage of me, and said I couldn't possibly be ready for marriage, I refused to bow down to their discouragement. I married him—and the blessing of his unending love, his belief in our family, and his willingness to embrace self-sacrifice has made an indelible mark on my life. In the moments when I felt God calling me to write *One Light Still Shines*, I battled negative self-talk surrounding my writing ability and the fear of condemnation from others, but I followed His lead and wrote anyway. And the book became a healing path for me and so many who have read it. When our family decided to pursue international adoption, some told us we already had too many children to handle another, and others told us to adopt domestically. Still, we knew God was drawing our hearts to South Africa—and our son has forever changed our lives. And when I tried to talk myself out of going to college, God continued to press it into my heart. Even though my academic advisors thought I was taking on too many classes each semester with inappropriate expectations, I did it anyway—and I celebrate God's perfectly timed process.

I can do hard things (I've proven this to myself). I can trust God to meet me in the hard place, and it's okay if others don't understand. I don't need another's permission to pursue the dreams and goals God births within my heart. I don't need to justify or explain anything. I need to fight for the blessing. And if I get off track, God will help me correct my course. He is kind and compassionate. His love never ends, but it doesn't mean I automatically get to return to the things I missed and receive those blessings. When I've chosen to settle, I've missed out on the experiences, relationships, and other gifts God intended. I refused what He offered and turned away. When I settle, the reality is I'm saying no to His gift, and there's no guarantee I will have a second chance later.

When I settle, I've given away my future based on a lie. I choose to believe in doubt instead of the beautiful partnership that happens when my ability mixes with the God of the impossible. We miss out on discoveries (about ourselves, others, and God), we miss out on the growth that comes when we pursue something we haven't done before, and we miss out on the opportunity to see the way God will come through for us. Do you remember what Jesus spoke to the father in Mark 9? He said all things are possible. I think about this scenario as if it occurred between myself and one of my children. Suppose Bryce had a dream for his future, but it seemed too big to him—he knew he couldn't do it alone. To achieve it, he and I would have to work together. We made plans. I knew my part, and he knew his. But one day, several weeks later, I realized he wasn't tracking with me anymore. I remained invested, but he didn't. When I asked him why he had given up on the dream, he said, "Well, Mom, I wasn't sure you'd stick it out with me." Those words, and their outcome would devastate me. He would have forfeited his opportunity, but it's more than that. If he thought I wouldn't remember, care, or follow through, his lack of belief in me would say something about our relationship. And it would crush me. I can only imagine this is how God feels when we do the same to Him.

I see the evidence of His steadfast love over and over. It's written through all the pages of my life. I can only be where and who I am now because of Him. And yet, when I'm settling, I'm saying to Him, "God, I know I can't do this on my own and I'm not sure I can count on You to stick it out with me, so I'm done." I don't think He would agree if I were standing face-to-face, having a similar conversation with Him. He would challenge me to identify where the thought originated. But when I'm deciding this in a split second by myself, I don't give Him the ability to interject, question, or challenge my beliefs. My settling silences Him. It's as if I've told Him I don't want to hear what He has to say because I've already made up my mind.

> When I settle, I've given away my future based on a lie. I choose to believe in doubt instead of the beautiful partnership that happens when my ability mixes with the God of the impossible.

I robbed God of the blessing He wanted to wrap around my life. And I denied myself the new season I desperately needed. And this becomes the place (and reason) I become cynical or resentful of God. In the weeks following my choice to settle, I begin saying, "God, why haven't You answered my prayer? Why am I still waiting? Where are You?" And then, in His endless kindness, He brings truth. "I did hear you. I did answer you. It isn't the season I chose for you. You chose this when you settled." And I know He's right. I don't want to do that anymore. I don't want to break His heart and miss out on the deepening relationship He planned. He counted on me to choose the blessings, but instead, I chose the lie.

And friends, I don't want you to do this either. We've missed out on opportunities which would've resulted in blessings for ourselves and those around us. We could have changed the world. But we dumbed down our impact, capability, and call because we chose to believe a lie of unworthiness, inability, and an unreliable God.

It's time to change our story. It's time to go back and embrace a course correction, endeavoring to make it the last time we purposefully put ourselves in this place. And it starts by acknowledging our need for forgiveness. We have yet to discuss *this* area of forgiveness—forgiveness when we've broken God's heart. And just as I would immediately embrace my son if he came to seek the same, God is waiting to welcome us. He's been waiting. He knows. "God, I'm sorry. I believed in a lie instead of fighting for Your truth. I sold myself and Your dream out over doubts and fears. I gave away the future You intended for me. Oh God, help me turn this around, bring me back on track. Don't leave me here in the middle of my defeat. God, I want to partner with You. I trust You. I believe You but help my unbelief."

As soon as we speak, He is moving. He comes close. He leans in, and He lifts our heads. He takes us by the hand and invites us to begin again. New opportunities may take time. God knows the right time, but in His mercy, we are always in the right place at the right time. He doesn't shame us for missing past opportunities or condescendingly show us what could have been. Instead, He invites us into a place of a renewed relationship. He helps us learn how to communicate with Him and find the confidence necessary to believe in the capabilities already within us. No expectations. Instead, we move with expectancy. We know God will meet us every day. He will make a way even when we don't see it. And as we learn to trust Him in the small things, God will start to help us find Him in the bigger things. We probably won't know it's happening, but He knows. God taught my broken heart how to trust Him after my daughter's death. Looking back, I don't understand how He did it. I just know He did. Perspective is everything, and I see Him as I look through eyes that believe.

Maybe you're wondering what it looks like to fight for the blessing. It's different every time. And it doesn't always feel like a battle. Sometimes our thought process *is* our battlefield, and the rest is easy once we choose to fight. Sometimes every step is agonizing. But He will make a way, even when it's a battle we never wanted, and we're sure we won't make it through.

I say this based on experience. Of all the stories I've shared with you, there's one I've yet to tell. In January 2019, God asked me to start the year by spending a quiet weekend away with Him. One of my friends has a quaint cottage in an idyllic location an hour north from my home. It was just far enough. I asked if I could use it for a weekend, and she said yes. The home was peaceful and felt like a sanctuary, a place of quiet away from the chaos of life with five teenagers. I eagerly anticipated what God would do, our conversations, and the clarity I'd gain through this weekend spent with Him. But it didn't unfold according to my plan. Friday night was everything I imagined. I journaled, read, sat by the fireplace, and soaked in the peace of nothingness. Saturday brought cold rain, so I stayed inside, perched on the window seat, looking out at the wooden shingles covered in moss, and watched the rain fall. I waited for God to bring clarity for the next season, but He was quiet. Late that evening my daughter texted to say she and her boyfriend had broken up. I felt relieved. There was something that just never felt right about their relationship. I went to bed hoping God would give me a dream or speak His plans for this next year in some way before I left Sunday at noon.

Instead, during the night, my phone rang. It was my daughter. She was upset and asked if she could come to see me. I was an hour away, but I could tell she was serious, so we met at a convenience store halfway between our home and the cottage, and she rode with me as we traveled back to my little sanctuary. It was there she told me she was pregnant. And I felt everything crumble inside of me. It was one of the conversations every parent dreads. I don't think I'll ever forget how scared I was. I thought about how hard it would be; I knew the kinds of things people would say, the sacrifices that would be necessary, and the way this would change her life. I told her we would do this together and she had the support of our family behind her. I prayed for strength and grace, but I felt weak. I held her as she cried. After we talked for a while, she went to bed. I tried to call Dan, but his phone was off. It felt like one of the longest nights of my life. Sleep eluded me. Fears and doubts plagued me. I kept thinking about the coming change and the condemnation she'd endure from those who criticized her choices.

And if I could go back and encourage myself in the early hours of knowing, I would say, "It is going to be okay. Actually, it's going to take your breath away—these next months will be an amazing journey. You're going to see God move all the obstacles. No, it won't be easy, but it will be more than worth it. Set your fears aside because it's going to bring some of the best moments of your life. Don't give authority to your doubts. Stand firm on your hope in God. He won't disappoint." I can't imagine life without my grandson Lincoln. I had to choose to fight for the blessing, and most of the fight was (at least initially) in my head. But I'm grateful for the words God spoke and the way He challenged and helped me so I could help Abigail.

Sometimes when God asks us to fight for the blessing, it's going to look like something we wanted, and sometimes it's going to look like the very thing we'd give everything to avoid. But regardless of circumstance, it is more than worth it when He invites us into the fight. Lincoln has changed my life. He is full of laughter. Unfortunately for everyone else, I'm his favorite, and I can't imagine anything more beautiful.

Chapter 15
Shine Your Light

The final stage of transformation comes when we cannot keep the impact to ourselves, we must share it with others. And often, we are entirely unaware of the deep purpose and passion that comes in the process. It happens as we read an acquaintance's social media post. Something rises inside of us. They feel lost, isolated, and devastated. They feel like their life is out of control, and the moment we read their words; we know we must respond. We have walked a similar journey. We understand their pain and must tell them they are not alone.

We send an encouraging message, which turns into meeting up for lunch, texts throughout the next week, and then a meaningful friendship. And sometimes, as we use our pain to pave the pathway for someone else's healing, we experience a marvelous surprise. Along this pathway, we uncover the beauty we missed in our earlier journey when we were lost in our brokenness. We've been down this road before but back then, we couldn't see the vibrant flowers that carefully lined either side of the path. But now we see our past with fresh eyes. We still see hardship, but we also see beauty. As we lead our friend down this road, we talk about how God met us, and suddenly we flashback to our inaugural journey.

This time, we see the way He walked with us. It's as if we are transported back to our hard season but we see it through *His* eyes. He was so close. We could've reached out and touched Him. We are overcome with emotion as we watch how tenderly He met us along the road. We tell our friend how close He is. We encourage them to reach for Him and believe He is with them. We tell them they are never alone, forgotten, or abandoned. And we feel it with a conviction and passion we didn't feel before. In the middle of welcoming them into a place of hope and healing, we journey deeper into ours. And while it may feel like it cost a lot to get there, the price we've paid is less significant when we can give others what we've found. As our time together ends, we walk away knowing we want more moments like these. And not because we want them for the value they brought us, they were personally powerful, but for the hope they infused in our friend.

One singular experience changed us, and we'll never be the same. We actively look for those who remind us of who we were "before." We seek out the ones who radiate discouragement. We identify with them, and we are drawn to them because we were once just like them. I feel these moments during women's conferences, Zoom call with my coaching clients, while exchanging messages with new friends on social media, over coffee chats with others like me in my community, and while writing this book. And you will find your version of these moments too. Women excel at creating community. Now, more than ever, we need others to link arms and walk with us. You can light the way for someone desperately trying to exit her darkness. She can't do it unless you shine bright and lead the way.

One of the themes contained within these pages offers an opposite perspective. Isolation is at the core of so many struggles I faced. Isolation negatively impacts our mindset; it strengthens negative self-talk and increases self-sabotage. Isolation makes it almost impossible to go after our dreams, develop resilience, identify our strengths, and break our goals into manageable pieces. And if there's one thing we all experienced throughout the pandemic, it's isolation. According to the American Psychological Association, "lack of social connection heightens health risks as much as smoking 15 cigarettes a day or having alcohol use disorder."[4] Loneliness and isolation reduce immune function. It increases the risk of premature death, mental health disorders, and dementia. Ongoing or extended loneliness can become a chronic condition with a greater risk of adverse impact. The APA notes, "Chronic loneliness is most likely to set in when individuals either don't have the emotional, mental or financial resources to get out and satisfy their social needs or lack a social circle that can provide these benefits." Trauma isolates us, and the isolation can become long-term unless we already have a strong support system. We struggle to fit in with the friends who used to feel so comfortable.

Even years after the pandemic, we have yet to return to the level of social interaction we enjoyed pre-2020. We need meaningful relationships; it's not optional. Loneliness and isolation negatively impact our physical, mental, emotional, and spiritual well-being. In each of the struggles I've shared, I felt alone. While we can still use our tools to help us process, heal, and recover from any obstacle, the context of a relationship increases life experience. Instead of starting the process by looking for someone who will become our friend, we can look for those who need our friendship. Reach out to the first person who comes to mind. Don't second-guess yourself. It's as simple as sending a message of encouragement.

While I used to spend excessive amounts of time agonizing over the words God spoke to my heart, my response is more immediate now. As I witness the transformation that happens in others when I share my experiences, it has increased my desire to do more of it. God's ability to write a beautiful story is not dependent upon me. It rests on who He is and the way He can take my nothingness and create a transformation. He doesn't expect me to be perfect. Instead, He asks me to participate from a place of trust.

But I often wonder what life would look like if I approached every goal, dream, and plan from a place of certainty—believing there was no way I would fail because that's the reality. When I partner with God, there is no failure. Sure, there are moments where I learn and circumstances I see differently, but there's no failure. There isn't one story in the Bible where God called anyone a failure and dismissed their impact. However, there are moments when He could have made that decision. But He didn't see them as failures, and it's not how He sees us. And God isn't waiting to partner with us until our life looks like something we would deem a success. He doesn't see us or our circumstances as failures or successes. God sees us through His eyes of love, His desire for us to discover the treasures deep within, and our limitless capability. He can use us at any point (and every point) along our journey.

Something tangibly miraculous occurs when we discover the way our brokenness gives us eyes to see the pain inside another. As we begin to experience healing, we can offer hope to others. Just as you've found hope through this book, you can share your hope with others who struggle. Pain is pain. It's not a competition, and you don't have to have walked out the same path to be able to offer relevant help. Authentically sharing your story with another is one of the greatest gifts you'll ever give. As you embrace authenticity and invite them into your secret and sacred space, you pour courage upon their weariness. They will find hope in the knowledge you haven't given up. We need to know we're not alone. We need to build relationships with others who have walked a similar journey and survived.

Two of my closest friends were single moms with stories like Abigail's. They are intelligent, strong, and capable women. Knowing them gave me hope and belief that Abigail's story would include similar content. Their husbands are some of Dan's closest friends. They have vibrant families. They are authentic about their past, courageously speak hope into others, and know how to ignite strength in place of weakness. They live like Jesus. They intuitively knew what we walked through in a way most others missed. They were my safe space. I could talk about our experiences, even the most difficult parts, without hesitation. Their friendship gave me hope. Their stories gave me confidence, and their authenticity lit up the darkness in front of me.

When I partner with God, there is no failure.

And it's what we do as we share our stories with others. We shine a light into their darkness. But we must first allow God to light us up. We must make space for Him to birth a passion so deep we won't walk away when the days are complicated, and we don't see progress. What's the dream that comes to mind even now? What's the thing that has come back to you repeatedly over the past few months or years? And what's the first step along your path? Often our passion comes because of our pain, and we discount ourselves as if the brokenness we've known is a hindrance, but in fact, it's a blessing,

As our family moved through the adoption process, I remember feeling like all the loss we knew was a strike against us. As if it made us less desirable, but I was wrong. It was the opposite. Our family knew how to navigate pain, and we understood how to blend and create a family. Our kids could identify the loss our son knew in the early years of his life. The pain I'd endured as I helped my kids grieve their father prepared me for the grief that comes with knowing my son had lost his mother and father. Our wounds were not disqualifications. Instead, they were advantages.

We knew and saw things that would've been hard to learn from a book, but life was our teacher. The lessons, strategies, and insights we learn from life experiences are often far more profound than what we understand by reading someone's stories or methods within a book.

Your experiences are not disadvantages; you are not less than others. You are not flawed or second best. Instead, your pain has enabled you to speak life to the broken and hope to the hopeless. And you don't have to go on a mission trip to make an impact. Others like you live in your community, and they need you. They need your friendship, your insight, and your encouragement.

So, what is your next step? Do you need to embrace your pain and allow God to walk with you on a healing journey? Do you need to challenge your doubts, silence negative self-talk, and end the self-sabotage? Maybe you need to refresh your confidence in your self-worth, or perhaps you need to find God. Wherever you are, embrace it. Give yourself the grace you need for this part of the process. Don't despise your starting point. Refuse to compare yourself with anyone else. Choose to believe this journey holds breathtaking moments and a surprise ending! God has created this adventure for you, and you deserve to live it!

You have the tools you need to navigate every obstacle you face, but you don't have to do it alone. A strong support system is one of the best gifts you can give yourself. Maybe you need new friends or deeper friendships. Pursue them because those people need you too. Seek out a mentor, coach, or counselor. Surround yourself with those who will tell you the truth—not just the words you want to hear.

Allow God into all the cracks and crevices of your life. Find Him in nature, in others, and in yourself. He's there, and He's waiting for you to find Him. If you feel like this whole God thing is just something you do because you're supposed to, then set aside the things others told you and allow Him to speak something else, something more.

Take a moment for reflection. Take some time to pause and write down what's impacted you most. My goal is not to move you to the end of this book as quickly as possible, especially not in this final chapter. Here, in this place, I don't want you to read it and move on. I want you to respond to the things stirring within you. Transformation comes when we take the time to engage in our places of impact. So many times, I've read a great book and had every intention of implementing the insights gained, but I didn't stop long enough to reflect and determine my next step. So the good intentions I had evaporated, and I missed the opportunity to live a life changed by those words. I want you to experience what happens when we step out of our Americanized expectation of constantly moving to the next thing. The magic happens when we decide not to move forward into our next project but instead allow God to saturate us in what we've just received. We come away with the determination of our next steps. It's where we come alive.

What does it look like when you feel vibrantly alive? When it's just you and God, who are you? What is the dream you want most? Sit with Him in the development of these questions—it's your first step. You may have to go backward to move forward. Maybe it's been so long since you felt vibrantly alive that you don't even know how to describe it anymore. And friend, there's no shame in admitting it. We all find ourselves in seasons where we are completely lost, disconnected, and isolated. But we don't have to stay there. I find my place of becoming vibrantly alive through wonder, creativity, huge goals, and serving others. Get to know yourself, identify the things that bring you joy, and incorporate them into your daily life. Remember the activities you enjoyed as a child, teen, or young adult. What were your hobbies when you had fewer demands and more free time? What is the thing you keep telling yourself you'll do when you finally get a break? We can't wait until we think we have enough time. Instead, we must rearrange our schedule and block off time for ourselves. When I engage in activities that spark my creativity, it positively impacts all areas of my life. I smile more, I'm less serious, and I enjoy my daily routine in a way I can't when constantly moving from one task to the next.

In each concept presented in this book, one common denominator makes all the difference, and it's us. We *are* the difference maker. Yes, we need the tools we gain through psychology, and we benefit from a relationship with God, but even with those things, if we don't use the tools, they won't make a difference. Simply having the tool doesn't guarantee success. I can collect a wide array of power tools and put them on the shelf in my garage—things like a cordless drill, circular saw, and belt sander, but they provide no benefit on the shelf. It's only when I use them that they make an impact. And it's the same for us. We can know about mindset, understand the importance of positive self-talk, and learn steps to resilience, but unless we practice them or intentionally institute them in our lives, we stay the same. We can hear stories about God, feel inspired by the ways He came through for another person, and receive an invitation to partner with Him, but unless we act on the opportunity and build a relationship, we won't benefit from all He offers.

We all face obstacles. Most adults experience some form of trauma throughout their lives, and simply knowing something won't enable us to overcome it. We must intentionally use the knowledge we've gained, but we can't just do it once. We must constantly remind ourselves to adjust. Otherwise, we'll find ourselves settling, embracing negative self-talk, and proclaiming we've reached our limits. One thing we need to ensure we don't give up is grit, and it's woven through the context of each previous chapter. Dictionary.com defines grit as "firmness of character;

indomitable spirit." If someone is indomitable, they "cannot be subdued or overcome." When you pair the two definitions together, it becomes a firmness of character that cannot be subdued or overcome. And it is precisely what we must embody to remain steadfast in our resolve. It's what enables us to overcome any obstacle.

Grit shows up when we refuse to back down, give in, or change course. While I didn't know it then, when I look back over my life, I feel the grit left over in the aftermath of the Amish schoolhouse shooting. I see it in my decision to marry Dan, our family's determination to pursue an international adoption, my resolve to graduate with a 4.0 GPA, and even in the way this book came together. Grit says no matter what the circumstance suggests, we will continue to fight, pursue, and believe in the possibility of a positive outcome until the bitter end. We are the fight. And friends, it's time to embrace it.

> *You didn't read this book because you were curious about the title. You read it because you desperately desire change. There are obstacles in your life standing between you and your destiny, and you can overcome them one step at a time.*

One of the highest compliments I've ever received was from an acquaintance who said, "Your grit is gritty." Angela Duckworth is a pioneering psychologist in the arena of grit, and she defines it this way, "Grit is passion and perseverance for long-term goals."[5] She suggests grit doesn't rely on a specific reward but focuses on a goal you pursue even when you don't see progress. Grit comes from the combination of perseverance and passion. Grit is a commitment to an outcome. And according to Duckworth, women are grittier than men. We all can demonstrate grit and live it out, but often, we don't know how to do so, or why it is essential. Many women grow up with cultural or religious influences that encourage submission. And so, when we find ourselves in the middle of traumatic or difficult circumstances, we revert to our upbringing and submit to them.

No one told us not to submit to the struggle. We're not telling our girls to fight. But, friend, that's exactly what I'm saying. Fight with everything you've got. Embrace grit and live it out. Become the grittiest possible version of yourself. Esther was gritty. So were Ruth, Deborah, and Rahab. The Bible includes the stories of many women who, perhaps unknowingly, embrace passion and perseverance for their long-term goals even when there are no short-term rewards. I love using rewards to reinforce motivation, when possible, but sometimes there's no reward big enough to compensate for the circumstance. When my goal was to create a normal and meaningful life for my family, defined by hope and faith in our future, the reward *was* accomplishing the goal. But it's difficult to say when I would reach a point where I could identify those conditions existed. It took grit to get up every morning, work through my responsibilities as a single mom, and take small steps toward my goals. There was no relevant, short-term reward.

> There's nothing we can do to make Him love us more and nothing we can do to make Him love us less, because His love is not dependent upon us. It all rests on Him.

Grit takes you where talent, socio-economic status, and education can't reach. It changes the trajectory of your life and becomes the most direct path to your goal because it demands focus. Grit and resilience work together. And we're better able to pour ourselves into them when we've reframed our mindset, conquered our negativity, overcome our trauma-based thinking, given ourselves permission to dream, developed our relationship with God, and fought for our blessing. It's all connected, and it's necessary.

You can do it. Look at how far we've come together. I believe in you. You didn't read this book because you were curious about the title. You read it because you desperately desire change. There are obstacles in your life standing between you and your destiny, and you can overcome them one step at a time. I know you've got what it takes. In those moments when you begin to doubt yourself, come back to this chapter. You must encourage yourself. Yes, you can lean into God and your support system, but you must choose to do it and believe in all that exists within you. Dreams are waiting for you. There is a future not defined by your past. Yes, we will always look back and remember the events from our past, but we'll also see how far we've come.

It's time to shine your light. You're not insignificant. You matter, and everything inside of you has value. Jesus came because He loved us—every single one of us. You can give others that which you always wanted to receive. Your brokenness does not have the final word. God brings dead things to life. There's nothing we can do to make Him love us more and nothing we can do to make Him love us less, because His love is not dependent upon us. It all rests on Him. Let Him love you. Let Him light your life, and then let it shine.

Your Invitation:

So, what is your next step? I can't wait to hear about it. Send me an email or find me on social media. Friend, you only need to take one step at a time. We don't need to see the whole equation; we don't need to know every detail. All we need to do is take the first step, and yes, the first step is often the hardest. You have the tools, and you know the shortcuts. You can take my mistakes and skip over them. You can do this. If I can make it, so can you. We haven't reached the ending; this is where your story begins.

Conclusion

Some of my favorite childhood memories involve spending time with my dad listening to episodes of Paul Harvey. I especially enjoyed hearing him say, "And now, the rest of the story." Every story has a backstory. I enjoy the process of back-tracking, uncovering the easily overlooked moments that lead to an outcome. These moments are crucial. While they're not usually the ones we look at, nod our heads, and acknowledge it's what made the ending possible, without the small but significant steps we wouldn't arrive at the endpoint. Throughout the process of this book, those moments filled my life. So now, friend, I share "The rest of the story."

My first book, *One Light Still Shines*, was published in 2013. Since then, I have often asked God when I would write a second book. There was more to share, and I couldn't set aside the belief that I would, one day, tell more of the story. But as the years passed with no definitive reply from God, I questioned myself. There have been seasons when I thought it was finally the right time, only to realize (partway through a writing process) I was wrong. In the past few years, I had convinced myself I probably wouldn't write another book. And then, I went to college, which became the perfect practice zone (unbeknownst to me).

When God spoke this project into being, I felt it. It was powerful, and it captivated me. As I walked with Bruno that afternoon, the concepts, details, and time frame unfolded in my mind. When I returned home, my goal was clear—finish the initial rough draft by October 31, 2022. Later that evening, I jotted down some basic chapter titles and focus. The following day I sat on my porch and figured out my daily action steps. I needed to write about 2,000 words/day, five or six days each week, to accumulate the approximate word count, and finish by the end of October.

And then I began working—and it was work. Some chapters flowed easily, while others were a seemingly endless struggle. I wrote between coaching clients, around time with my family, first thing in the morning and late at night. From the outside, my days didn't look like they held the blocks of uninterrupted time necessary to make this happen, but this is the way God works. He takes our nothingness and transforms it. When I felt stuck, I took Bruno for a walk, AirPods in, and music playing. When the internal pressure increased, I released it and embraced God's call to live freely and lightly, inspired by Matthew 11:28–30 (MSG).

> "Are you tired? Worn out? Burned out on religion? Come to me. Get away with me and you'll recover your life. I'll show you how to take a real rest. Walk with me and work with me—watch how I do it. Learn the unforced rhythms of grace. I won't lay anything heavy or ill-fitting on you. Keep company with me and you'll learn to live freely and lightly."

I thought about the invitation to walk with God and work with Him through the unforced rhythms of grace. Unforced. This one word became my anthem. I couldn't force it. Instead, I had to find the rhythm of grace, even when it was the opposite of what I would typically choose. These rhythms and this grace carried me when I doubted my ability, was overcome with emotion, and as unexpected circumstances took me away from writing.

I thought I would miss the deadline. In one week, I went from pacing ahead to falling far behind. I was still coaching, consulting, speaking, and trying desperately to stay present as a mom and wife. I pressed into the concepts I wrote about and practiced them with more conviction than ever before, and they worked. I finished one day before the deadline. This process works. I mean, I know it works, but I watched it unfold before my eyes.

> *Here's the thing: there is more for us. We deserve to dream, to wonder (with eager anticipation) over the future God designed. But first, we must believe we're worth it.*

And I began to understand why the book couldn't come until this season of my life. I needed what I learned in college. The psychology and theology classes deepened what I knew. The hundreds of written pages and the positive feedback from my professors gave me the skill and confidence necessary to conquer my goal. (And you'll read more about their impact in the acknowledgments.) I couldn't have done it without them. I needed the experiences, perspectives, and struggles gained in each new season of my journey. I needed the lessons life offered and the opportunity to walk through the almost decade that's passed since my first book. God knew. It may sound cliché, but it's not—His timing is everything.

Thank you, friend, for embarking on this journey with me and for allowing me to share my stories, advice, and challenges with you. We all need tools to help us overcome obstacles, but sometimes we also need help finding the tools. We need someone to help us, but we don't know who to trust. We want to believe

God loves us, but we don't know how to make belief fit around the brokenness in our lives. We desperately want to dream about the brilliance coming on the horizon, but we're scared dreaming will only lead to more disappointment. And so, we take all these doubts, fears, and questions, and we surround ourselves with them as if they protect us from future pain. But it isolates us and becomes our prison cell. We convince ourselves we deserve this cell and it's all God intended for us. We release the hope of a bright future and settle into the darkness.

And while it works for a while, we get tired of the misery. We're tired of the pain. We are tired of using all these tools that seem sufficient but aren't helping. Things like wine, chocolate, and endless scrolling on social media, checking out while we binge-watch ten episodes of a new season on Netflix. We're just trying to escape the reality that is suffocating us, but our escape is only temporary. And reentry into our reality is almost more challenging when we return than before we left. We're tired of fighting despair, comparing our lives to everyone else's, and always coming out with the short end of the stick.

But here's the thing: there is more for us. We deserve to dream, to wonder (with eager anticipation) over the future God designed. But first, we must believe we're worth it. We deserve a life that fulfills us to the point we don't compare ourselves to others or self-medicate with chocolate, wine, or our screens. But we can only find this kind of life if we walk out of our prison cells, break ties with our negative mindset, and choose to redefine our lives.

And we can do this whenever we're ready. It happens through embracing the strategies that offer real change. It comes by partnering our faith in God with psychology—utilizing tools while embracing an outrageous, indomitable commitment to ourselves. You have permission to go after the life you want. You have my support in all you take on. And when God whispers something that lights you up—pursue it without hesitation. If He can take five weeks and turn it into a book, He can do anything. And then, when you achieve your goal, it's time to set a new one. The process continues because God continues to create.

If you're still holding on to the comfort of your cell, here's my invitation—come out. Take my hand; let's do this together. It's time for me to begin again, which is also the perfect time for you to join me. What do you have to lose? Let's start writing your story.

Acknowledgments

Wes Yoder: Thank you for fighting for me, this book, and the lives it will touch. I'm grateful for the way you've walked with me throughout the past decade.

Amanda Varian and Lisa Parnell: It was a joy to work with you. Thank you for helping me share the impact of *To Help You Heal* with the world.

Kristen Ingebretson: You took my cover inspiration and exceeded my expectations! Thank you!

Sr. Laura Downing: Thank you for seeing and calling forward the capability inside of me.

Sr. Sheila Galligan: You find beauty and promise within each person you meet. You are dynamite, and I'm grateful for your presence in my life!

Professor Aronovitz: You gave me the courage to believe in myself, set aside my fear of failure, and release the words inside me.

Professor Dunn: You helped forge the connection between what already worked for me and the principles that work for everyone. Thank you for being the conduit between experience and learning.

Dr. Maria Cuddy-Casey: You changed my life with one sentence: "You should check out our Organizational Behavior major." Thank you for seeing attributes in me that opened the door to purpose, impact, and fulfillment.

Leanne Sia: You helped me own my powerhouse vibe. You're a cherished coach and friend. Grateful for you!

My SUPPLY Church Family: You'll always be my "home church family." You allowed me to be myself and provided an atmosphere rooted in authenticity while etched with possibility and purpose.

My Elevated Members: Thank you for allowing me to walk with you over the past few years. I cherish your feedback and encouragement. Your vulnerability and courage are inspiring.

Cindy Templeton, Cyndi Coakley, & Theresa LaCesa: You were some of my first coaching clients, but you've also become treasured friends. Thank you for loving this book and championing its impact!

Sandy Diller: You care deeply, intentionally, and consistently. You are one of the most self-sacrificial people I know, and I'm forever grateful for your friendship.

Dawn Sweigart: You speak the truth in a way that brings focus, intention, and action. Your faithful friendship and love have changed my life.

Shawn & Kelli Cutting: You have a way of listening, understanding, and supporting that births hope, especially on the hard days.

Mom: Thank you for loving, serving, and feeding our family in all the ways you've always done, but are such gifts in this season.

Bruno: My faithful walking buddy. You were with me when this project ignited in my heart, and you took each step with me through the finish line.

My Little Bean: You showed me what it's like to live and love in a way I couldn't see until you came.

My Kids: The best part of my life is being your mom. You're my teachers, testers, and triumph. We've come a long way, but *your* best is yet to come.

Abigail & Bryce: Thank you for allowing me to share your stories. Walking through life with you has enabled me to be a better version of myself. I couldn't have done any of this without you; you inspire me.

Dan: You believe, serve, and love in a way I've never known. Thank you for embracing each task I threw your direction while writing this book. But more than that, thank you for choosing this adventure. You are everything.

Notes

1. "How to Manage Trauma," National Council for Mental Wellbeing, https://www.thenationalcouncil.org/wp-content/uploads/2022/08/Trauma-infographic.pdf.

2. "Trauma," American Psychological Association, https://www.apa.org/topics/trauma#:~:text=Trauma%20is%20an%20emotional%20response,symptoms%20like%20headaches%20or%20nausea.

3. Harvard study "Human Flourishing Program" as found at Everett L. Worthington Jr., "How Hope Can Keep You Happier and Healthier," *Greater Good Magazine*, June 17, 2020, https://greatergood.berkeley.edu/article/item/how_hope_can_keep_you_happier_and_healthier.

4. Amy Novotney, "The Risks of Social Isolation," American Psychological Association, May 2019, https://www.apa.org/monitor/2019/05/ce-corner-isolation.

5. "What is grit?" in FAQ at https://angeladuckworth.com/qa/.

Made in the USA
Columbia, SC
15 March 2025